Working-Class Women and Grass-Roots Politics

Working-Class Women *and* Grass-Roots Politics

Kathleen McCourt

 INDIANA UNIVERSITY PRESS
Bloomington & London

Published in Canada by Fitzhenry & Whiteside Limited, Don Mills, Ontario

Manufactured in the United States of America

Library of Congress Cataloging in Publication Data

McCourt, Kathleen.
  Working-class women and grass-roots politics.

  Bibliography
  1. Women in politics--Chicago. 2. Discrimination in housing--Illinois--Chicago. 3. Labor and laboring classes--Chicago--Political activity. I. Title.
HQ1439.C47M3 1976   301.5'92'0977311   76-26340
ISBN 0-253-36650-X

Contents

Working-Class Women and Grass-Roots Politics

Introduction

Women have been called "the silenced majority"; working-class women have been characterized, as "absent from the majority" altogether.[1] The kinds of public policies and social structures which could serve the needs of working-class women by making their lives and those of their families healthier, more productive, and less fraught with anxiety and insecurity do not exist. Working-class women have been without organized voice and certainly have been absent from the consideration of those who make public and corporate policy. But there is increasing evidence that their silence is coming to an end.

So far, women with blue-collar jobs either have been totally unorganized or, if in unions, have been excluded from the leadership and unable to push for their own interests. This may change substantially if groups like the Coalition of Labor Union Women (CLUW) which was able to draw over 3,000 women to its founding convention in 1974 continue to grow in strength. Working-class women in their communities have also been unorganized, both with respect to issues that affect them specifically as women (for example, abortion and divorce counseling, credit and insurance discrimination) and issues that affect them primarily as members of the working class (for example, inadequate housing, poor school and health facilities). There are

3

changes here, too, but gradual and so far very slight. This book looks at the experience of some women who have been involved in trying to bring about such changes in their own neighborhoods.

I first became interested in the relationship between working-class women and the problems in their communities in 1971. I had a general and unfocused interest in how the working class was responding to the political events of the 1960s, specifically the movements for civil rights, peace in Southeast Asia, and women's liberation. As I began looking through sociological and political science literature on the American working class and its politics, I was struck by the absence of data on working-class females. What little there was portrayed working-class women as uninvolved, housebound, and apolitical.

At the same time, my attention was becoming more focused on the working-class neighborhoods of Chicago and I became aware of the new and increasingly militant community organizations that were gaining constituencies in those neighborhoods. Some of the most involved, articulate, and visible participants in those organizations were women. The evident contradiction between my observations and the academic literature inspired me to explore further what was going on.

Since that time in 1971 when I first set out to fill some of the gaps in my personal understanding and sociological analysis of the lives of working-class women, others have embarked upon similar endeavors. There is now a far richer body of literature on working-class women than there was five years ago, although by almost any other standard it remains sparse. A few of these works deserve explicit mention.

Much of the new research on working-class women focuses on the workplace. Pamela Roby, Robert Bibb, Sally Hillsman Baker, and Mary Lou Finley are among those who have examined various aspects of women's work.[2] A survey by Social Research, Inc. has updated many of the findings they published twenty years ago on the attitudes and values of working-class women.[3] Nancy Seifer's monograph of a few years ago touches on a range of spheres--job, family, community--and has found a wide audience and triggered discussion groups in New York and Chicago.[4] A more recent book by Seifer, <u>Nobody Speaks for Me</u>, recounts oral histories from ten working-class women around the country, vividly depicting the conflicts and promises that have resulted from the reconciling of past lives and contemporary crises.[5]

This new research is important. Not only is it adding to an historic and contemporary understanding of working-class women, it is also correcting some of the inaccuracies in the traditional social science treatment of this group. The omission of working-class women from academic research (and popular writing as well), when it has been acknowledged at all, has been justified on the grounds that they never do anything noteworthy and they certainly have not been political.

Like other people, working-class females have, over the years, grown up, married, had families, worked, struggled, and grown old. The days of working-class women are filled with meeting the demands of family, household and, often, job, but the relationship of women to these integral aspects of their lives has not been seen as important by social analysts. The energies of many working-class women are absorbed in struggling for decent housing and food for their families and decent education for their children, and in trying to reconcile the contradictions of a capitalist system that demands consumption of unnecessary goods while making the attainment of life's necessities-- health care, clothes that last, food without harmful side effects--increasingly problematic. But this behavior has not been defined as political.

One of the effects of the women's movement over the past decade has been a social redefinition of what is political. "Sexism underlies our conception of politics. . . . It has taken the feminist challenge to redefine many questions, previously considered strictly private, as political issues."6 Being able to get a job, a pay raise, a credit card, or an abortion are for many women no longer seen as personal problems but are defined as part of a political struggle.

This book does not present a final portrait or provide any definitive analysis. Rather, it attempts to give some insight into changes that are taking place in the lives and political consciousness of some women, and to further a bit our collective understanding.

There are a few preliminary comments I would like to make about this work. One of the hypotheses motivating this research was that participation in the process of political change through the direct action tactics of assertive community organizations would have an impact, politically and personally, on the participants. The expectation was that the participation itself, regardless of whether the issue that inspired it was progressive or reactionary, would, to some extent, have similar consequences for all who took part. Organizing with like-minded neighbors to put pressure on intransigent public agencies and private businesses in order to gain some control over events in their communities is likely to produce feelings of frustration, cynicism, efficacy, and anger in the membership of both liberal and conservative groups.

Nonetheless, the effects on participants of such activities will not be totally the same regardless of the issue involved. There are areas in which the ideological orientation of the leadership and the nature of the issues around which struggle is waged will have differential effects. Participants' development of an analysis of how the political system

works will be largely dependent on how victories and defeats are interpreted. Whether
people are fighting to retain the status quo or
to improve the quality of their lives, who is
defined as the enemy and who are perceived as
potential allies--these will depend on both the
issues and the leadership and, according to how
they are interpreted, will be capable of moving
constituencies in different directions.

It is unfortunate that the number of respondents and the restricted range of ideological concerns that they reflect have precluded
here the kind of analysis that would take into
consideration the different ideologies of the
groups. I point this out because it should be
made clear that the absence of this kind of
analysis must be attributed to empirical
restrictions, not to any denial of its importance.

I feel it is important to raise here the
issue of racism which permeates any discussion
of the Southwest Side of Chicago. The Southwest
Side has been perceived as racist by many who
live outside the community at least since 1966,
when Martin Luther King was jeered and stoned
while leading a march for open housing through
the area. Typically, black families moving into
its fringes are verbally harassed and often
physically attacked. A branch of the American
Nazi Party has headquarters in the community
and, led by a handful of neofascists, periodically holds rallies and marches. While few
residents openly support Nazism, these rallies,
intended as a show of force to keep blacks out
of the community, are sometimes attended by
hundreds. A recent march, drawing upwards of
400 participants, featured a large group of
white male teen-agers wearing "white power" T-
shirts and carrying "Nigger beware" placards.
Such incidents sustain the community's reputation as racist and in the case of some
individuals, that label is warranted.

Despite their lesser visibility, most

Southwest Side residents abhor the tactics of Nazism and violence and condemn those behaviors in their neighbors. Yet, they share a fear of integration and feel personally threatened by the possibility that blacks will move into the neighborhood.

A knowledge of Chicago's pattern of segregation is a prerequisite for fully understanding the panic of white families. Chicago, characterized as the most segregated city in the North, has failed to create genuinely integrated neighborhoods. Each year blocks of houses on the South Side and the West Side, previously occupied by white families, become the homes of black families. All the white families leave. "There is no such thing as integration; it's always resegregation" was a comment I heard frequently, and census statistics bear this out.

In the face of this history in Chicago, racial panic is widespread. The families on the Southwest Side feel caught in the inevitability of that change and powerless to stop it. They are angry that they will have to transfer their children to another school, sell their homes, and move from a neighborhood they have loved. "But," one might say, as I said, "You don't have to. Don't panic and sell and it won't have to be that way. You can have a slowly integrated neighborhood." They would respond, as they did to me: "Show me where it's been different. Show me where it's worked."

As owners prepare for a quick sale, property is not maintained; Catholic schools close as their white constituency moves away; public schools become overcrowded. The cumulative and demoralizing impact of all this, the constant harassing tactics of realtors, and fears of inter-racial conflict are overwhelming and more than most families can take. Before I finished my fieldwork, two women I talked with in the early stages of interviewing had already moved farther west.

Race was a topic which occurred inevitably

in the course of each interview. I do not know
how accurately I was able to probe the racial
sentiments of these women, or how open they were
likely to be with a comparative stranger and,
worse yet, a sociologist. Nonetheless, it is my
impression that the organizationally active
women, while often displaying evidence of racial
prejudice, are no more--and perhaps somewhat
less--prejudiced than most other Americans. The
comparison of their racial attitudes with those
of a national sample in Chapter VIII (Table 25)
bears this out.

       Most of the women I talked with were begin-
ning to focus their blame and anger not on the
black families seeking to move into a community
offering better housing but on such institutions
as school boards, real estate companies, local
lending institutions, and the Federal housing
agencies. To the extent that the groups to
which they belong have been able to orient their
membership away from blaming victims and towards
doing combat with the institutions that control
housing, schools, and money throughout the city,
they have been successful.

       It may, of course, be argued that organi-
zationally active women are not less racist but
simply more adept at veiling racism, more
skilled at articulating sophisticated racial
positions that have the same concrete effect of
keeping the neighborhood white. I think this is
true, just as it is true for most middle-class
individuals. I also think, however, that most
of the women I talked with exhibited some level
of tolerance and some willingness to accept at
least a minimal level of integration. I have no
way of knowing how typical or atypical of
Southwest Side residents these women are.   I
also readily acknowledge that theirs is hardly
the most progressive position on integration.
There is, however, on the Southwest Side a world
of difference between those who are hard-core
racists willing to go to the barricades to preserve the alleged superiority of the white race
and those who express a willingness to attempt

to live and work within the context of certain
inevitable racial changes.

Some women worked in organizations whose
programs I respected; some worked in organizations about which I was ambivalent; a few worked
in organizations I would wish out of existence.
With most of the women, I enjoyed spending time;
with a few, I established warm relationships
that have persisted over the years; a very few,
I disliked.   In other words, they, like other
women, are all kinds of people and their organizations, like those in other communities, represent all kinds of tendencies.   And I have
responded with a range of emotions and judgments
which I readily acknowledge.

An additional point about this research:
while it is specific to a particular community
in a particular city, the nature of the problems
it addresses and the ways of responding to them
are not limited to the Southwest Side of
Chicago.   White working-class families who live
in the cities of the Northeast and Midwest in
the 1970s share a similar fate.   They are generally not in a position to move to the suburbs
where the housing is beyond their financial
means.   Consequently, housing available in the
city will be competed for by both blacks and
whites.[7]   Such families increasingly feel themselves victimized by city budgets that increase
taxes to the breaking point but do not provide
the basic services families need, such as
schools, parks, and hospitals.   It is not only
Chicago's white working class that faces this
dilemma.   And it is not only the white working-
class neighborhoods of Chicago that have responded to this dilemma by organizing assertive
community groups.   The same holds true in parts
of Boston, Baltimore, Cleveland, and New York.
Similarly, the dilemmas of the women who speak
in these pages are not unique: all women and
men who live in a society which perpetuates
privilege for the upper classes while simultaneously dividing the working class along lines
of   race   share   their   situation   and   their

struggle. While this study, then, is a case
study, highlighting the idiosyncratic features
of one community, it is also an example of a
phenomenon which is repeating itself throughout
the country.

The large number of tables found in this
book are intended to enlighten, not confuse.
They are often useful for a quick grasp of the
magnitude of differences in responses. Nonetheless, it should be clear that the sample is
small and differences which appear great should
not be taken as significant in a statistical
sense.

Finally, I would like to thank a number of
people who helped me in the various stages of
formulating ideas, carrying out fieldwork, and
writing what was first a dissertation and is now
a book. Thanks are due to the Center for the
Study of American Pluralism at the National
Opinion Research Center for financial support,
provided in part by Ford Foundation Grant No.
710-0070A. A special debt of gratitude is owed
to the Pluralism Center's director, Andrew M.
Greeley, who provided important support with his
consistent belief that the project would reach
completion. Others in the Center were also important sources of constructive criticism and
support: Barbara Currie, David Greenstone,
Ellen Sewell, William McCready, Shirley
Saldanha, Virginia Reich, and Julie Antelman.
James Davis, former NORC director now at
Dartmouth College, and Morris Janowitz, of the
University of Chicago, provided helpful suggestions.

Mary Lou Finley and Sally Haimo have been,
over the years, important to the development of
many of the ideas expressed in this work. I
thank them for their intellectual stimulation
and personal encouragement at the very earliest
stages. At later stages, Warren Friedman, Amy
Bridges, Kathleen Schwartzman, Barbara Currie,
and Alene Bycer read and commented on the manuscript. As they know, I took their feedback--
both negative and positive--with great appre-

ciation. I am also grateful to Irene Edwards
who typed the final manuscript with just the
patience and concern I needed at that point.

I wish to express special thanks to the
women of the Southwest Side of Chicago. For
their openness and willingness to give of their
time to answer my inquiries, I am grateful. I
hope that in my reconstruction I have produced
no distortions and in my analysis I have done
them no injustice. The confidentiality of our
relationship is respected; no names or identifying information are attached to the quotations. In their efforts to make governments and
corporations responsive to their needs, I wish
the women of the Southwest Side strength and
forbearance.

[I]

Women of the Working Class

The angry rumblings of America's working class, described by some as the emergence of the silent majority, grew increasingly louder in the late 1960s and by the middle of the next decade had become a strong and steady voice. Dissatisfaction with the direction in which the country was moving, skepticism about the real interests and honesty of those who hold power, feelings of abandonment by those who allocate resources, and dismay at governmental priorities--all these generated anger among men and women of the working class and lower middle class, an anger that spurred them to abandon their designated role of silence and give voice to their discontent.

Social analysts speak of "the silent majority," "the forgotten Americans," "the troubled Americans," or "middle America."[1] All these phrases refer to the same group of citizens, the multitude of Americans who live somewhere between poverty and affluence, the millions of women and men who make up the white working class and lower middle class in this country, the people who in the 1960s came to realize the discrepancy between their dream of America and the reality.

The increasingly evident discontent and anger of such large numbers moved many observers to concern as the potential for social conflict intensified:

The feelings of neglect, the sense of being less important in the minds of 'the establishment' . . . and the resultant hostility cannot be dismissed. They may not be accurate perceptions, they may not be as desperate as the feelings of even less privileged groups, and they may contain elements of prejudice and racism--but they are real, they are painful, and they may lead our nation into social conflict.[2]

Fed by such feelings of neglect, the first outbursts of anger that received attention from the wider society were indeed the kind of reactions, directed at those groups who seemed to be getting more than their share of attention from the government and the media, that contained the seeds of racial and cultural conflict. The famed Wall Street clash between "hard hats" and young war protesters and the 1969 Pittsburgh walkout of white construction workers to protest the demonstration of black workers against the small number of jobs they held with the construction industry typified such hostile reactions.

Over time, however, these kinds of confrontations between the white working class and others equally victimized by social practice and governmental policy have proved to be sporadic. They still occur--witness the violent 1975 racial clashes in Boston and Louisville over the use of busing to achieve racial integration in schools--and they still represent a blend of bigotry and legitimate resentment. But more significant, more accurately directed, and more lasting kinds of responses began developing in the 1970s.

On the national level, white working-class women and men in metropolitan areas, long-time mainstays of the Democratic Party, began reconsidering their political loyalties. During the 1968 and 1972 Presidential campaigns George Wallace's appeal to white urban dwellers in the North posed a serious threat to the Democratic Party. In both 1968 and 1972, Richard Nixon,

the Republican Presidential candidate, found
unexpected support in traditionally Democratic
communities.   The   shift in voting   patterns
in 1968 was enough   to lead one   political
analyst to speak of a "new Republican Majority."3 Watergate, Nixon's resignation, and the
ensuing series of revelations of governmental
duplicity in one agency after another turned the
tide   once   again   and   Republicans   lost   the
majority support they so briefly held.   There
was, nevertheless, a lesson in the voting patterns of the last decade: great numbers of
American voters are dissatisfied with the per-
formance of elected officials and cannot be
counted on to respond along party lines as they
have in the past.

     Along with the fluctuations in national
political alliances, and perhaps of more lasting
consequence,   there have been new political
developments on the local level.   In many
working-class and lower middle-class neighborhoods, men and women have started to organize in
order to confront directly what they see as the
sources of their frustration and anger.   "A
small but growing number of [immigrants'] de-
scendants are organizing to deal with the
multitude of problems in white working-class
communities.   The old 'intermediate agencies'
that once took care of their demands--the
political machine, the church, and the patronage
system--are fading from the scene or no longer
work effectively."4   In response to the anger,
the demands, and the declining effectiveness of
the old agencies, these neighborhoods have
witnessed the emergence of what can be called
assertive community organizations.

     These are grass-roots organizations formed
around problems shared by community residents.
They can be seen as part of "a national movement
for local control."5   In Newark, the Italian-
American community organized to assure themselves equitable political representation; in
Forest Hills, a largely Jewish working-class
community, residents organized (unsuccessfully)

to protest the construction of public housing in
their community; in Gary, a community group in
operation for only two weeks forced the City
Council to repeal an ordinance that had allowed
United States Steel to pollute the air with
impunity; and in Chicago, groups have come together to protest the building of an expressway
and to attempt to reverse the apparently
inevitable racial changes in the neighborhoods
of the Southwest Side.

There is no evident single political direction: some groups espouse typically "liberal"
or "progressive" causes, such as combating industrial pollution; others assume "conservative" or "reactionary" causes, such as opposing
the economic and racial integration of neighborhoods. What these groups share, regardless of
political orientation, is resentment toward and
frustration with elected representatives,
corporate executives, and bureaucratic officials who evidence little concern for or responsiveness to the needs of the neighborhood.
Accompanying the resentment and frustration is a
gradual realization that the traditional
institutions to which people with problems had
turned in the past--primarily the local church
and the local politician--are now parts of much
larger, much more disinterested structures. And
those local institutions and their representatives that may have retained some concern for
and contact with the community have lost
whatever power they once had to make themselves
heard.

It is within this context that residents of
working-class neighborhoods, forced to consider
alternative channels and structures, have begun
to shape and work within assertive community
organizations. These assertive community organizations, an outgrowth of the resentment and
frustration experienced by whites in their
neighborhoods, are very self-consciously taking
their cue from the civil rights movement of the
1960s and are using tactics of direct confrontation and mass demonstration similar to those

used by black groups in pursuit of their goals.

In the process, the white working-class housewife, historically considered one of the least likely candidates for political activism, is developing a political style similar to that of her poor sisters who have marched for welfare rights and her college-educated sisters who have marched for passage of the Equal Rights Amendment. In many of these new assertive community organizations, still struggling for strength and direction, women offer important leadership.[6] Often, too, women are the most active and most numerous rank-and-file members. All along women have been supplying the bodies for demonstrations; they are now beginning to make decisions, speak publicly, and assume more responsible positions in the organizations.[7]

Such active organizational participation constitutes a new and multifaceted role for these women. It is the expression of political sentiments which are a direct result of years of frustration, deception, and perceived victimization. In this sense it is clearly a political role, an attempt to realize certain community goals by persuading decision-makers to legislate or enforce policies amenable to those goals. Such activity is an exercise in power in the most basic sense: it is an attempt on the part of certain individuals to carry out their will despite the resistance of others. The resisting others may be citizens' groups with opposed interests, corporate executives, government agencies with established routines, or political leaders representing entrenched interests.

For the women involved, this new political role appears to have an additional dimension. It is an extrafamilial role which some working-class women not ready, inclined, or able to enter the labor force may play as they emerge from a world of conventional sex roles and male-female relationships into one where relationships between men and women are slightly less bound by tradition.

The sociological research on working-class women, while limited in quantity, is uniform in theme: the roles working-class women have been able or encouraged to play have been few. The working-class woman--especially if she does not hold a paying job--has not felt herself to be a part of any world wider than that of her family. Her daily life has been "centered upon tasks of home-making, child rearing, and husband servicing."[8] Beyond her immediate family, her friends and contacts in the wider world have been limited. She has not belonged to clubs or participated in groups, either formal or informal. She has tended neither to "coffee klatch" with her neighbors during the day nor to entertain friends at home in the evening. Her best friends have been members of her own family "less through choice than by virtue of [her] social isolation from any other kinds of people."[9] She has turned to television for companionship and stimulation; only housekeeping and caring for husband and children supersede watching television as a regular daily activity.[10] Perhaps more than any other single trait, social isolation has characterized the life of the working-class woman.

This, in brief, is the picture of a working-class woman's life which emerges from those works--Mirra Komarovsky's and Lee Rainwater's--which have, for years, been accepted as the definitive works on the subject. Such a picture is not accurate today. Whether or not it ever was is questionable. Women have participated in and supported labor strikes for decades.[11] They were a major force in 19th century neighborhood uprisings.[12] And they have had intimate if not extensive relationships with others in their community.[13] It is difficult to believe that working-class women have ever been the passive, isolated people they are portrayed to be. However, as with so many aspects of women's lives, there is no history which recounts for us the experiences of working-class women of the last generation in their communities.

It is well to keep in mind that both Komarovsky and Rainwater did their research in the early 1950s, the post-World War II period that was characterized by a withdrawal from work and politics on the part of many women as their husbands returned home and "normal" life resumed.   Betty Friedan documents the almost desperate flight to the home on the part of many women.[14] It was a flight encouraged by doctors, psychologists, and political leaders.

> Modern woman's participation in politics is through her role as wife and mother, said the spokesman of democratic liberalism [Adlai Stevenson]: "Women, especially educated women, have a unique opportunity to influence us, man and boy."[15]

The women Komarovsky and Rainwater talked with are women who came to their roles as wives and mothers in such a social and political climate. There is no particular reason to think that their behaviors and values characterize working-class women of other eras. In any case, a generation has passed. The women who participate in assertive community organizations in the 1970s are the daughters of the women of the 1950s.

The primary extrafamilial roles available to American women are those of paid employee and volunteer worker. The fact that more than 31 million women are in the labor force[16] and approximately 22 million women are serving as unpaid volunteers[17] indicates that these roles are popular ones for American women today.

Many working-class women work outside the home: nearly 49 percent of married women whose husbands earn between $7,000 and $10,000 were employed in 1974.[18] This is somewhat above the national average of 43 percent. For these women, obviously, social isolation is less pronounced. Still, half of this group do not hold jobs. Many working-class men object to their wives' working. The belief that this reflects negatively on a husband's ability to provide for his family is still strong. Problems of child care often stand in the way of work as well: a wife's assuming a job may either impose an additional economic burden as the family pays for baby-sitters or leave the children without adequate care.   Finally, there is the woman's realization that the jobs available to her, work in a factory or as a sales clerk, have little intrinsic satisfaction.   Consequently, wives who can afford not to work often do not, or they work sporadically, usually when there is a financial emergency.

The role of volunteer worker, which has a long history among middle-class women whose family income does not necessitate their working for pay, has never been very popular among working-class women.   A number of reasons for the class-specific nature of volunteer work present themselves.   Middle-class women have more education to prepare them for the kinds of work that charitable, educational, civic, and religious groups do.   They also have more money for household aids, baby-sitters, and second cars to free them from their homes.   Working-class women, on the other hand, have neither the financial resources to free them nor the education to provide them with the confidence necessary to deal with the professional and upper-middle-class women and men who staff the organizations which seek volunteers.

Working-class women, and especially those who do not have jobs, have lived in a social situation marked to some extent by loneliness and limited contacts with the wider social environment.   Often their major point of contact with the outside world is their husbands.   And, typically, working-class men are not very eager to spend time talking with their wives when they get home, tired from their jobs.[19] "Few workers talk much to their wives. They have little to say about their jobs . . . and little common meeting ground.   Unlike most middle class men, they have interests, tastes, and experiences often very different from their wives."[20] So the working-class woman finds herself in a situation where she is "excessively

dependent on her husband for contact and attention" and, as a result, "has a fairly steady
sense of frustration and disappointment because
his interests are such that he does not provide
these."[21]

This discrepancy between the interests of
men and women produces disappointment and frustration in women despite their realization that
this is "the way things are." Men and women are
not expected to share each other's interests and
activities. Neither sex explores or anticipates
understanding the feelings of the other.
Komarovsky cites cases in which she found "a
gulf so wide that neither [marriage partner]
could serve as a satisfying audience to the
other. They repeatedly missed the cues and,
when they did understand the other's concerns,
found them trivial and boring."[22] Men and
women are expected to inhabit distinctly separate social and psychological worlds.

The working-class woman, according to the
sociological literature, faces an inherently
unsatisfying situation. She is dependent on her
husband for contact with the wider world, but
her husband tends to be uncommunicative and not
to share her concerns. There is little wonder
that working-class wives express greater
discontent with marital communication and
closeness than do their husbands[23] and that a
study of the mental health of Americans arrived
at the conclusion that "the wives of unskilled
workers are perhaps the most deprived of all
women."[24] This study went on to explain that
much of this deprivation derives from the fact
that "their channels of expression are, for the
most part, limited to their homes."[25]

Within the framework of traditional politics, working-class women have played a restricted role. Historically, ethnic communities have had a unique and intimate relationship
with the big-city political machines. But for
most residents, male and female, this has been
largely a passive relationship, one in which
they have been at the mercy of the political
system. Those from the ethnic neighborhood who

have been able to advance personally or have in some other way actively manipulated the political machine to their own advantage have not been women.

In working-class communities, the allocation of interests and activities into sex-appropriate areas is strong, and politics has been "men's business." Elinor Langer, recounting her experience of working for the telephone company, speaks of the way in which political discussions are restricted to men's departments:

> The effect of the pressure of work and the ethos of niceness is to defuse political controversy [among the women]. There is a kind of compact about tolerance, a governing attitude which says, "Let's not talk about religion or politics." During the time I was there I heard virtually no discussion of Vietnam, the city elections, or race. . . .

> This is not characteristic of the men's departments of the company where political discussion is commonplace, and I believe the women think that such heavy topics are properly the domain of men: they are not about to let foolish "politics" interfere with the commonsensical and harmonious adjustments they have made to their working lives.[26]

A distrust of the political system is evident among large segments of the working-class population, male and female alike. "Working-class people everywhere believe, or know, the police to be crooked, and politicians corrupt. . . . Researchers have described the working-class antagonism toward law, government, and politics."[27] These feelings exist despite, or perhaps because of, the history of working-class families' dependence on the largesse and favors of the political machine.

Within this political context working-class females develop little sense of political efficacy, but rather the "exaggerated sense of deficiency in political or social efficacy which the subordinate partner in a subordinate family will have. . . ."[28] Occupying a social status

which combines disadvantaged class and sex positions, these women have had little opportunity
to nurture the belief that they can effect
change on either the national or the local political scene.

In the past, working-class women have been
less likely to join voluntary associations than
either their husbands or women of the middle
class. Sexton attributes this to a tendency on
the part of the working-class woman to avoid
rather than approach the world outside her
home. "She seems to lack the inner re-
sources--the self-direction, the confidence,
the assertiveness, the will--to move about more
freely in the larger world."[29]

In Rainwater's study, many women explained
their lack of group participation in terms of
the group's not approaching them. "I'd like to
join, but I'll wait until I'm asked." "I'm not
in any clubs because I don't know anyone who
belongs to introduce me."[30] The need for
friendly contacts to welcome people into new
social situations, of course, holds true for all
people, but the fact that there are fewer organizationally active people in working-class
neighborhoods has meant that women living in
these neighborhoods have been less likely to be
part of a social network which includes potential contacts.

In addition, the circumstances that make it
difficult for some women to take a job--the lack
of resources to free them from home and responsibilities and the absence of feelings of personal competence--make them reluctant to join
local organizations. Researchers arrive at the
following conclusion: "There is nothing 'collective' about [the working-class woman]; she is
basically unorganized, a central quality of her
life."[31]

It is important to note here that while
working-class men may belong to more groups than
their wives, they too are basically non-joiners.
Booth finds that, although men belong to more
groups than women within each class group, both

sexes in the working class belong to fewer
voluntary associations than their middle-class
counterparts.[32] This suggests that participation in assertive community organizations is a
role altogether new to the working class, not a
previously male role being adopted by females.

This is by no means to say that organized
life has been completely absent from working-
class neighborhoods. Certain kinds of voluntary
associations have constituted an important part
of ethnic community life.[33] Primarily they have
filled a social need, introducing people from
the same native land and providing them with
familiar recreational and social activities.
They also filled an economic need, making available to families both insurance policies and
immediate assistance in financial emergencies.
Finally, they filled an assimilative need,
helping immigrants "learn the ropes" of life in
a new and unfamiliar city. The ethnic voluntary
association, while it did constitute a special
interest group whose political support was
sought by candidates for public office, did not
initiate demands on the political system. In
this sense, the assertive community organization whose raison d'etre is to make the political system respond to it is a new social structure. And action within the organization,
constituting assertive and avowedly political
behavior, is a new role for the participants.

The literature on the working-class woman,
then, lays great stress on her limited involvement in the world beyond her family and on the
social and emotional deprivations she experiences. It emphasizes that she is resigned to
this reality, seldom expecting more from life
than what she has. At the same time, what also
comes through in much that has been written on
the working-class woman is her desire to experience more and to undertake more--a desire which
is hampered by lack of personal resources and
social supports. Sexton notes, for example,
that while the working-class woman is resigned

to her life as it is and does not expect more,
she often wishes for more than she has--more
companionship, more excitement, more freedom.
"There is usually at least a wistful longing to
break out and a well-founded suspicion that they
are missing something important."[34]

There is some evidence that, with encouragement and the opportunity to do so,
working-class women are willing and eager to
enter into organizational life. "Often, when
these women, with their bottled-up needs for
expression, are let loose on an organization,
they show an almost breathtaking eagerness for
activity."[35] The behavior of women in assertive
community organizations demonstrates just that
kind of enthusiasm and intensity as they move to
bring about desired changes in their own neighborhoods.

Methodology

Because the political activism of working-
class women, and indeed their political consciousness in general, is an unexplored phenomenon, this work constitutes an exploratory
study. It utilizes in-depth interviews with a
limited number of carefully chosen women. The
analysis is intended to provide an initial step
toward understanding the dimensions of this
political role as it is being experienced by its
participants.

The term "working class" as used here refers to a family where the head of the household has a blue-collar job or a white-collar
job of relatively low salary and status. Married women, traditionally, have been assigned
to a class on the basis of their husbands'
jobs. This is reflected in the titles of social
science works such as "The Wife of 'The Happy
Worker'" and Workingman's Wife. The sociological inadequacies and ideological biases
of such a male-centered approach are evident.[36] Nevertheless, there is a logic in
looking at the household as the social class

unit of analysis. The economic and social
fate of women in this society is strongly
linked to the jobs and salaries of their
husbands.[37] Married women with paying jobs
contribute only about twenty-five percent to the
total income of families earning between $7,000
and $14,999.[38] Constraints on full-time work,
the existence of a dual labor market which re-
legates most women to lower paying job sectors,
and discrimination in wages within sectors keep
women to a great extent dependent economically
on men.

　　　The women chosen to be interviewed lived in
selected white neighborhoods which, on the basis
of census data reflecting median family income
and percentage of male workers in professional
or managerial jobs, could qualify as working-
class neighborhoods. The median family income
in the selected neighborhoods averaged approximately $11,500 in 1970, somewhat more
than that for the city of Chicago as a whole,
$10,280.[39] Thirteen percent of workers were in
professional or managerial jobs, compared to a
Chicago average close to 18 percent. The remaining 87 percent of workers hold blue-collar
or lower level white-collar jobs.[40]

　　　Neighborhoods on the Southwest Side of
Chicago were selected because, in addition to
their working-class characteristics, they have
been the breeding ground for a number of new
assertive community organizations and the participation of women in these groups has been
highly visible. The selected neighborhoods are
virtually all white. The decision to limit the
sample to white women was based on two factors:
1)the history of the black woman, her family,
and her community is sufficiently different from
that of the white woman, even when they share a
social class position, that it would be difficult and probably misleading to treat both as a
single group; and 2)while in many instances
black and white community organizations share
similar problems and sometimes even work together, in other instances--and this applies to

f activity is an important variable.
is occurs, the activity groups are
separately.

order to see how the attitudes of women
in assertive community organizations
from those of women who are not so in-
an additional sample of women who were
ve was interviewed. The non-active wom-
ing from the same community, had been
to the same sorts of community problems
e living in the same social context, at
ith respect to community environment. Al-
these women were designated non-active,
a reference only to their lack of in-
nt in assertive community organizations;
y, of course, be active in other spheres
er groups. Seventeen non-active women
terviewed.

e interviews averaged several hours in
There was an interview schedule which
as a guide, but respondents were en-
d to voice whatever came to mind in the
of the discussion and were free to
the feelings and attitudes behind their
es as much as they wished. Because the
ents were free to explore their own par-
areas of interest, there was some
on in the topics discussed with each
ent. Consequently, when attempts are
attach numbers to the qualitative data
onsideration in this book, those numbers
ry from one topic to another. All the
ews were recorded on tape; no one
d to this procedure. Verbatim tran-
were made to preserve intact the words
en used and the context in which they
them.

though the issues receiving attention
from one respondent to another, there
number of areas which were covered, at
to some extent, with each woman. These
1)feelings about the community in which
ed; 2)assessment of the problems facing
munity and how they were being responded

some of the groups under
white identity and the fa
class are important moti
organization and its part

Once the community h
necessary to locate the po
assertive groups.   These
marily   through   an   inves
local newspapers. Several
to the investigator since
been receiving a good dea
An   attempt   was   made   to
varied on issues and po
The criteria used in sele
the   following: the   org
community-based and loca
Side of Chicago; it had tc
the political system; it h
action tactics, such as pi
strations,   or   confron
officials; and it had to
controversial in the commu
of the fieldwork, women
assertive   community   orga
interviewed.

Two kinds of women ma
of the sample, those who w
those who were "somewhat a
designated "very active" i
or   more   politically
organizations and either w
of those groups or attended
per month.   A woman was
active" if she belonged
oriented   community   organi
officer, and attended no m
per   month.   Seventeen   wo
"very active"; six were
active."   In   much   of   t
follows, these twenty-three
sidered a single, active gr
the two groups display bel
which differ noticeably an

level
When   t
treated

In
active
differ
volved,
not act
en,   co
exposed
and we
least
though
this i
volveme
they ma
and ot
were i

T
length
served
courag
course
explai
respon
respon
ticula
variat
respon
made t
under
will
inter
object
script
the w
placed

varied
were
least
were:
she l
the c

to by public officials; 3)her organizational
memberships; 4)attitudes toward the local and,
to a lesser extent, the national political
system; 5)political behavior; 6)attitudes
toward women's roles in general and in politics
specifically; 7)attitudes toward integration;
8)attitudes toward the social class structure;
9)ethnic background and attitudes toward ethnicity; and 10)demographic information. In addition, those women active in the assertive
community organizations were questioned about
the extent and nature of their involvement.
Interviewing took place from January to July of
1972.

        The two chapters which immediately follow
are intended to provide a context for understanding the behavior of the participants.
Chapter II discusses the women's community, its
history, and its problems. Chapter III sketches
an outline of the women themselves, their personal histories, and what their lives are like
now. Chapter IV begins to look at the women in
their role as community activists and to attempt
to understand what led them to get involved and
what has been the impact of that involvement in
their personal and political lives.

[II]

The Community:
The Southwest Side of Chicago

During the 1972 school year, a major struggle between Chicago's white Southwest Side community and the adjoining black community took place around the issue of overcrowding at a local high school. Spokespersons for the white parents claimed that it was not a racial issue, that they were concerned only with the fact that the school was operating beyond its capacity while nearby high schools had empty seats. Black parents and students, on the other hand, definitely saw the issue as a racial one; after all, the "extra" students who would be forced to leave if enrollment were cut back according to the white community's plan were all black. Over 1,000 white students boycotted the school for ten weeks; picket lines and counter-picket lines of parents and students marched outside; sporadic fights broke out between white and black students. When the students finally returned to school, tight security measures were put into effect for the rest of the year. No solution satisfactory to all parties was reached and the school year went on in an atmosphere of highly charged racial tension.

On the Southwest Side, an issue like this can inflame the entire community. The conviction that neighborhood integration quickly follows school integration is firmly held by the

30

residents. Fear of integration is always present; the anger and anxiety surrounding that
fear rest just below the surface of this white
community's smooth daily functioning.

Such fears have been a part of this community at least since 1966. It was in the summer of that year that Dr. Martin Luther King,
Jr., led his famous march for open housing
through the Marquette Park area of the Southwest
Side and was met with catcalls, obscenities, and
rock-throwing. King later claimed his reception
on the Southwest Side of Chicago was the most
vicious and violent he had experienced in any
part of the country.

After King's march, the community's anxieties crystallized and its reputation for being
racist and resistant to change solidified. In
the years following, residents of the Southwest
Side have done little to dispel the idea that
they are totally unreceptive to integration.
Neither have the city's officials done much to
assuage the anxieties and fears of the residents
of these white neighborhoods.

While the incident at the high school was
in many ways another example of the fears and
hostilities that had triggered the attack on Dr.
King, things did change in the years from 1966
to 1972. King's march appears to have marked an
important turning point in the history of the
community. People in the area became frightened
that summer, some at the possibility of blacks
moving into their community, others at the potential for violence evident in their white
neighbors. Some liberal clergymen, along with
the more moderate elements of the community,
attempted to pave the way for eventual racial
integration through education and organization.
People opposed to integration also began to
organize; they became more deeply entrenched in
their opposition and more active in their resistance.

The following years saw the development of
new and aggressive community organizations, and

it is in these groups that the women of the community are finding a new political role. While
King's march was a major impetus for organizing
and concerns about integration remained paramount, organizations in the community began
eventually to address themselves to other issues
as well. A brief history of the Southwest Side
in the years following 1966 provides some perspective for understanding the environment in
which these organizations have developed.

The Southwest Side is primarily a residential community, lying south and west of
Chicago's downtown. There is a small amount of
industry in its northeast section and along its
western boundaries, but essentially the
Southwest Side is a community of neighborhoods,
with bungalows and duplex homes, neighborhood
stores, and many schools and churches to meet
the needs of its large families. Family structure is traditional: the man is the head of the
household and the major breadwinner. Many of
the men work for the city as policemen, firemen,
or maintenance workers. Sometimes, to make ends
meet or in response to a family emergency, the
woman in the family will take a job, usually
working in an office or as a sales clerk.

The residents are second- and third-
generation Americans, products of European ethnic stock, primarily Catholic. For years, the
community was composed of numerous small ethnic
neighborhoods. To some extent this remains true
today: Polish, Lithuanian, German, and Italian
neighborhoods with their own bakeries, grocery
stores, and restaurants can still be found. But
by and large the various ethnic groups have
moved into one another's neighborhoods and in-
termarried; most residents will now describe
their community as ethnically mixed. Still,
families are not far removed from their European
origins. Many have parents or grandparents
living in their homes who speak only broken
English. The comforts in their lives, especially their homes, are of relatively recent
acquisition and so are jealously guarded.
Before the last few years, the only community

organizations with any following, other than churches, were the "homeowners' associations." The more recent immigrant groups appear to be the most active and vocal in these homeowners' associations. It is due at least in part to the tenuous nature of their recently acquired property and comforts that racial change is such a persistent fear to the residents of the Southwest Side.

The heart of the Southwest Side is all white. But black families are beginning to move into blocks along the eastern edge. As this happens, white families move further west. It is not unusual to find white families that have moved two or three times to "escape" racial change. In the border areas where change is occurring, racial clashes flare up periodically. Black families moving into a neighborhood have been met with violence in the form of fire bombings and rock-throwing. Many white families, too, live with fear--sometimes confirmed, sometimes irrational--for the safety of their children and their old people on once familiar streets.

Along the edge of the Southwest Side where racial change is occurring runs a chain of block clubs started by a Catholic priest, Francis X. Lawlor. Father Lawlor symbolizes both the racial fears and the independent political stirrings in the community. Lawlor's motivations in organizing the block clubs are described by community residents as everything from "racist" to "Christian" to "crazy." Upon starting to organize, he quickly became the spokesman and the symbol for attempts to keep blacks out of the area. For this reason, in 1968, Chicago's Cardinal Cody exiled Lawlor to a boys' preparatory school in Tulsa, Oklahoma. Lawlor defied the order, returned to the Southwest Side to continue his organizing, and was subsequently stripped of his ecclesiastical powers. Although as of this writing he has not regained good standing with his church, Lawlor's followers continue to think of him as "a good priest."

Lawlor contends that his attempt has been to "stabilize" the community in order to prevent the occurrence of resegregation, that is, a complete shift in the racial composition of the area from all white to all black. Primarily, says Father Lawlor, the purpose of the block clubs is "to promote the cultural, social, and economic cohesiveness of the community."[1] He makes reference to "a European heritage" which white residents share.

The block clubs are clearly inspired by Lawlor's personal presence and guidance. In fact, Lawlor developed such a large and loyal following through his organizing that, in 1971, he was able to run for the Chicago City Council and win, defeating the incumbent Democratic alderman by an overwhelming two-to-one margin. As an alderman, Lawlor moved into a position where he could push for legislative and policy decisions to aid the goals of the block clubs. He had some few and mild successes: a city ordinance was passed making it illegal to display "For Sale" signs since these are used to generate panic in racially changing neighborhoods; the Department of Housing and Urban Development began an investigation into the granting of FHA (Federal Housing Authority) loans in Lawlor's ward.[2] Neither he nor his block clubs, however, seem able to stop the shifting racial makeup of the neighborhood. In fact, as racial change becomes defined as inevitable, the block clubs have become increasingly weak and ineffective.

Lawlor's successful candidacy for public office is an expression of the growing dissatisfaction with Mayor Daley and the Democratic machine which has characterized the Southwest Side in recent years. Lawlor ran as an independent and often lined up with the handful of other independent aldermen in the City Council who tend to oppose, although ineffectually, the proposals of Mayor Daley's Democratic aldermen.[3]

As further evidence of independent stir-

rings, two other Southwest Side wards had
Republican aldermen at the time of the interviews. These signs of dissatisfaction with the
established Democratic political system are
especially noteworthy in this community since
many of its inhabitants hold jobs with the city.
These workers and their families might be
expected to have some indebtedness to the city's
political machine and, consequently, some reluctance about displaying political independence. But sentiments like the following are
not   infrequently   voiced   by   residents:
"They [the Democrats] think they can always
count on us; they take us for granted."   Increasingly, it seems less true that these residents can be counted on to vote a straight
Democratic ticket, although Daley himself swept
the area in the 1975 mayoral campaign. (One
woman complains that no matter how much they
change their voting patterns, things remain the
same: "First they said, this is a great
Democratic bulwark that can be depended on, so
you don't have to do anything for those people.
Then when people started rebelling and put a
Republican in, you still don't have to do anything for these people because they elected a
Republican.")

     Along with the electing of an independent
and Republicans, the beginning of the assertive
community organizations signifies the dissatisfaction of residents with things as they are.
At the basis of the dissatisfaction is anger,
anger at not being listened to and anger at
having changes forced upon the community.

     The Southwest Side is a community conser-
vative in its moral norms and social behavior.
Throughout Chicago, this area is recognized as
being extremely resistant to change. In the
past, this has meant not being open to innova-
tions in the community. Child care centers,
mental health clinics, sex education programs,
and drug abuse clinics might get started, but
many such programs are short-lived; community
disapproval forces them out. In recent years,
more than passive resistance has been necessary

to keep change away from the community.   A
Federal court's decision to build public housing
units in these neighborhoods and a state plan to
build a Crosstown Expressway which will cut
through the Southwest Side have been, along with
the push for open housing and school desegregation, major changes that residents have resisted.   Because Federal and local governments
and courts have been behind these decisions,
only a well-organized resistance could effectively engage in combat.   Awareness of this has
been another factor moving the community to
organize.

A growing dissatisfaction with public
officials and the policies they are trying to
impose on the community along with an increased
awareness of the need to organize to be effective have transformed the Southwest Side into an
organized and aggressive community.   The
Southwest Side remains conservative.   But its
residents now realize that to maintain their
social order as it has been requires increasingly active behavior on their part.

While "Southwest Side" is a common term in
Chicago for a single community covering a large
geographic area, that community actually con-
tains within it a number of smaller neighborhoods, each with its own distinct characteristics, problems, and organizations. Here, too,
the Southwest Side will be treated as a single
community, but a brief summary of the differences among the neighborhoods and the history of
the community organizations may be useful.

The neighborhoods under consideration are
outlined in Figure 1, which divides them geographically into four areas: the southeastern
(Auburn-Gresham); the central (Gage Park, West
Lawn, Chicago Lawn, and Ashburn); the western
(Garfield Ridge, Clearing); and the north-
eastern (Bridgeport, New City, McKinley Park).
The neighborhood names and boundaries on the map
are those delineated more than forty years ago
by Ernest Burgess and his colleagues at the
University of Chicago. People's perceptions of

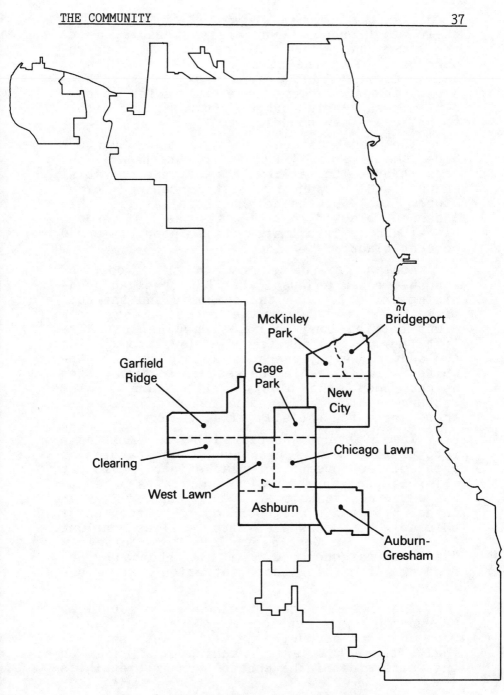

Fig. 1.   Map of Chicago showing selected
neighborhoods

their neighborhood boundaries do change, as do the names they choose to identify their neighborhoods.[4] But the names provided by Burgess, as it turns out, are familiar to the respondents. Because there were only a few respondents in each neighborhood, it was not possible to delineate new boundaries.

The southeastern part of the Southwest Side, the neighborhood of Auburn-Gresham, is the area referred to earlier as experiencing racial change and responding with organized block clubs. In 1960, the neighborhood was less than 1 percent black;[5] in 1970 it was 69 percent black;[6] and 1972 estimates ran to about 75 or 80 percent black.

Ashland Avenue runs down the middle of Auburn-Gresham and was, when Lawlor began organizing in 1967, both the symbolic and the real dividing line between the races. The block clubs battled long to hold the line, but have lost the war. Black families now live west of Ashland. However, there is no integration: the white families are in the western section of the neighborhood, the black families are in the eastern section, and, where the two groups meet, there are a few racially mixed blocks.

The Highburn Associated Block Clubs came into existence as a response to one particular problem, the movement of blacks into previously all-white neighborhoods. It was a response by the white residents to what they perceived as an invasion of their neighborhood. The section of this neighborhood where white families continue to live is, in Gerald Suttles' terminology, a "defended neighborhood,"[7] a neighborhood defending itself against intrusion from outsiders.

The defended neighborhood, says Suttles, is "primarily a reponse to fears of invasion from adjacent community areas."[8] Not surprisingly, then, this area, running as it does on the white side of the ghetto boundary, exhibits more of the traits associated with the defended neighborhood than any other Southwest Side neighborhood.

Fear is pervasive. There is a fear for physical safety, an uneasiness in the streets.

Ten years ago if I had a fifteen-year old daughter I'd let her go anywhere. Today I drive her. I pick her up. I won't let her walk down the street. It's just . . . maybe I'm being over-cautious . . . but I mean, in the daytime, yes, if she's with her friends, I let her go. I mean, I'm not that . . . but in the evening, if she goes to a basketball game, I'm sure we pick her up at 10:30. I don't let her walk home.[9]

There are many elderly people in this neighborhood, people who have lived here all their lives and now are afraid and do not know what to do or where to go.

We have a great number of older people in the neighborhood. They've retired and hope to live here until they die and they're just scared, you know. They lock their doors even during the day and they fear to walk to the corner. They're pathetic . . . they really are. They can't go out in the suburbs without any transportation and the cost of apartments out there.

Through the block clubs, a community safety force was established. Rotating details of men patrol the streets in cars equipped with short-wave radios with which they can contact the police department almost directly. But participation in the patrols is falling off. "The men are losing interest in going out every night . . . they got bored evidently and they felt as though they weren't doing a good job . . . or whether they were feeling as though it's a useless cause and the crime is still going to happen wherever they're not."

Other responses to fear mark this as a defended neighborhood: extreme security precautions on homes and stores ("like through the shopping area here . . . we have guard rails put up now around the stores so baskets aren't stolen and things like that. So many things

have changed like that"); sharp designation of
boundaries within which it is safe to walk
(several mothers point out that their children
are lonely, without playmates, because their
young friends are no longer allowed to walk east
to the homes of friends living closer to the
black community); police patrols in the elementary schools; and an attempt at restrictive
covenants.

The restrictive covenant attempt has been
through a referral service set up by the block
clubs. The organization attempts to find white
families to buy homes which go up for sale and
encourages white residents leaving the area to
put their houses on the referral list of the
block clubs rather than go through a real estate
agency. The professed aim of this service is to
maintain an integrated community in the face of
realtors' tendencies, in such a situation, to
sell almost exclusively to black families. The
actual intention of the referral service is to
take homes off the open market. In any case,
under the weight of the organized pressure of
the real estate companies and the massive shift
in racial population, the referral service has
been largely unsuccessful.

There appears to be another fear among the
white residents of this neighborhood. Although
less readily articulated than the fear for
physical safety, there seems to be some sense
among the women that in losing their community
they are losing whatever cultural identity remains to them.

The two public grammar schools in the white
section of the neighborhood went from 17 percent
black and 3 percent black respectively in 1967
to 79 percent black and 90 percent black in
1972. This means that each day, when the black
children come into the white residential area
where the schools are located, white parents and
children (like the black children) are exposed
to an alien culture. "I can't even understand
them," says one mother. "They have a whole different language of their own. I get 'man' and

'boy' from my own little one. . . . It's awfully
hard to get used to them in great numbers like
this all at once." So even before black
families buy homes, the white residents have had
daily contact with a culture that is foreign to
them.

Such fears of losing one's own cultural
community cannot be responded to as directly as
can fears of physical danger. Because they
cannot be so readily dealt with, such fears are
likely to be even more unsettling. There is no
programmed response equivalent to the security
precautions.

> You have a certain culture and maybe it's not the best
> culture in the world, but there's nothing wrong with
> it and then you're thrown in with a whole different
> type. . . . I don't think any people should be forced
> to change their way of living because other people
> are surrounding you and that's their way. It's not
> fair. Then you're really taking away your inalien-
> able rights to live the way you want to.

The block clubs association has been a
defensive organization since its inception. It
has had neither the time, nor the freedom, nor
perhaps the interest, to innovate and push forth
its own goals. Rather, it has been a reactive
organization. It came into existence to deal
with what were already crises in the community--
community safety, the practices of real estate
agencies, school conditions.

Over the past few years, the association
has put consistent pressure on the Board of
Education to change elementary school boundaries so that the threatened "resegregation"
would not occur. The pressure has consisted of
such actions as presenting personal pleas to the
Board at its monthly meetings, filing law suits,
picketing the schools, and lying down in front
of construction equipment which was being used
to set up mobile classrooms. The pressure was
not strong enough and, as indicated, these
schools are now virtually all black. The
association members contend that their pleas

fell on deaf ears because the Board of Education, along with other official decision-making bodies, had "written off" their area. They are the victims, they feel, of a self-fulfilling prophecy: everyone "knows" that this community will soon be all black, so no one takes any action to prevent this from happening and then, in a few years, the area is all black.

Another major issue for the block clubs in 1971 and 1972 was Federal Housing Authority loans. Many of the black families moving into the area, unable to finance their homes through conventional mortgage loans, are using special housing loans made available through the Federal Housing Authority. Many of the block club members oppose what they view as a proliferation of FHA-backed purchases in their neighborhood. They have made attempts to get Congress to take action to limit the percentage of homes in any area which can be financed through these procedures. Their contention is that FHA loans not only contribute to "resegregation" but also populate a neighborhood with residents who are financially unable to maintain the upkeep on their homes. Throughout the streets of the neighborhood, in block after block, practically every house has a sign in one of its windows which reads: "We're here to stay! Down with FHA!"

Women have played a markedly active role in the organization. While block presidents are typically men, everyone acknowledges that it is women who do the office work, provide bodies for the demonstrations, and are the backbone of the organization. The following statement appeared in the group's newsletter for August 28, 1970:

FOR WOMEN ONLY . . .

This article is addressed to "women only" due to an incredible fact. THERE ARE NO MEN LEFT.

It might be more correct to state that there are FEW men left. What do I mean? Attend any neighborhood meeting and tell me what gender is prevalent. Women, of course.

"But," you ask, "where are the MEN?" Good question--
just where are the men? Some are working, surely.
Some are sick in bed or in a hospital. Right! WHERE
ARE ALL THE REST?

"My husband works hard and long at his job."

"My husband is baby-sitting."

"My husband is cutting the grass."

Ladies, the list of excuses is endless. The truth of
the matter is, your "man" is not a man at all. True,
he is still of the male species, but any trace of
MANHOOD has vanished.

The truth of the matter is he's sitting on his "duff"
denying YOU, HIS CHILDREN, HIS NEIGHBORS, and HIS
COMMUNITY any talent that he may have in bettering
his, and your, surroundings.

MEN OF THE AREA--UNITE! Show us that you're really
out there.

Never fear, Ladies . . . THERE ARE NO MEN LEFT TO HEAR
THE CALL.

At its peak, the association had 93 blocks
organized. Fewer than half that number of
blocks remained organized in 1972. The decrease
is due primarily to the many white families that
have moved out. When an officer of a block club
moves, it has a particularly demoralizing effect
on the neighbors, as one woman explained:

One of the secretaries of our block club said she just
wanted to get an estimate on her home and the next
thing you knew, she was gone. . . . A week later, we
got a notice and her name was signed to the bottom of
it which, I said, is kind of a slap in the face.

This is a neighborhood already lost to its
white families. The fear, the distrust among
neighbors, and the rapid movement out of the
neighborhood attest to this. Whites who remain
continue to identify the area as their neighborhood, but their protestations that they will
remain no longer carry confidence. One woman,
even while insisting she would not move, inad-
vertently slipped into a verbal tense which
indicates she will: "My heart would be broken

if I had to move. It really will be. I don't
want to face it. It's something I keep putting
out of my mind."

Another woman who had at one point been
quite active in her block's organization sum-
marized the feelings of most of the community:
"I feel the block clubs were very successful in
that they stemmed the change, slowed it down. I
think if the block clubs hadn't been in existence, we probably would have been in this
situation three years ago."

This racially changing neighborhood is
unique on the Southwest Side because it is the
only neighborhood in which blacks do live.
Nevertheless, the changes it is going through
are the same changes feared by families living
further west. They see a re-creation of the
same problems in their own neighborhoods unless
they are militant in their opposition to blacks'
moving in. So there has developed throughout
the entire community an obsession with racial
change and an atmosphere in which anything new
in the community is viewed in terms of its potential for accelerating or slowing down ulti-
mate racial change.

The heart of the Southwest Side, the
central area, presents at once a picture of
complacency and anxiety. Many of the families
living here moved in when they had "made it."
"This is where people move when they get out of
Back of the Yards," explains one woman, "or when
you're buying your own home." Living here was
expected to be an escape from the problems that
had plagued them or their parents in earlier
years, and people wanted serenity and security
with their new homes.

The image of their community that many here
choose to present is a happy one, a neighborhood
not in the throes of any crisis, but just "nice,
old, comfortable." One woman tells why she
thinks it's a "fine community":

It's stable and it's made up of so many ethnic groups
and it's just marvelous the way they all get along.

Across the street from me are Lithuanian people and
next door to them are Irish. Next door are more
Italian and Polish; over here are Slovak; on the next
corner is another Italian family and a German family.
So we have a nice mix and we all get along, no
problems.

Residents of this area work hard at maintaining the illusion that they have no problems.
Mental health clinics, a program to deal with
drug problems, child care centers, and sex education in the schools have all been resisted by
people contending, among other things, that such
services are unnecessary in their community.
Many residents resent the government's providing any services for which they feel the family
should be responsible. They resent also any
implication that such unwelcome conditions as
mental illness and drug use might be found in
their families.

The "problem" they most strongly resist,
the one to which they most adamantly refuse to
accommodate themselves, is that of black
families moving into their neighborhood. This
neighborhood is all white, and vehemently so.
It was the scene of both Dr. King's march and
the high school incident discussed earlier. The
woman who spoke above of all the ethnic groups
living happily together went on to state rather
emphatically her intention of doing all she
could to keep black people out of the area.

Resistance to public health, educational,
or recreational services is sometimes openly
based on the fear that black people might come
into the community to make use of such services.
One woman, objecting to this attitude in her
neighbors, explained:

They wanted to put a pool in Marquette Park years ago.
They had a skating complex designated for the park.
Really great! The people said no. . . people didn't
want it because, after all, it's a public park,
right? And you put skating facilities over there,
and you put a pool over there, you know who's going to
come and use it?

While this neighborhood is not yet experiencing racial change, it is an eventuality that many residents believe is not far off. Already changes are evident: "We're starting to get, I've noticed in the last six months, these little real estate handbills in the door." And another woman speaks of watching "the signs [of change] in the neighborhood: empty store fronts suddenly, businesses that have been going for twenty, thirty, or forty years are leaving. It's just happening within the past few months."

Possibly this section of the Southwest Side will soon bear a stronger resemblance to the neighborhood to the east and more of the signs of a defended neighborhood will appear. Signs of change are becoming evident not only in the community but also in the residents. More and more, the people who live here are beginning to express anger at the extent to which they are ignored. "We're not a problem community," says one woman with some resentment, "we're a very nice, trouble-free community as far as downtown is concerned. . . . There's not a high crime rate. There's not a high unemployment rate. We have no problems that come to the notice of anyone." What appears to be a contradiction emerges: the residents feel ignored and yet they resist additional community services. Perhaps it is not a contradiction; they are not really asking for more services from the government, but for more attention.

In any case, contradictory attitudes characterize this neighborhood. The people are not of one mind. The John Birch Society and the American Nazi Party have offices here. The Common Counsel of Participating Organizations is a local community group with strong conservative tendencies; some of its more outspoken members oppose inter-racial marriage, sex education in the schools, and United States participation in the United Nations. At the same time, the Southwest Community Congress, a moderate organization which the Common Counsel opposes, draws strong support from the neighborhood. And the Southwest Committee on Peaceful

Equality, a group whose intention is to promote peaceful integration, is also located here, although its membership is small and its activities are few. Women from all three of these groups were interviewed.

The formation of the Southwest Community Congress (S.C.C.) can be traced directly back to King's march. After that encounter, in the words of one member, "the various clergy all got together and their decision was they would hire someone to come into this community and see what he could do to organize and help quell some of the fear."

After going through a series of organizational changes, S.C.C. held its first Congress in the fall of 1968. Approximately 500 delegates representing about 100 organizations--churches, schools, civic, business, and fraternal groups--attended. Liberal clergy were active in initially forming S.C.C. and church groups were heavily represented at that Congress. Partly as a result of this, S.C.C. came to be perceived by many residents as "integrationist." One woman explained: "The people out here think everything the church is involved in means integration. This is the biggest hang-up in the community."

While S.C.C. officers do appear to have a liberal political philosophy on most community issues, they have been careful not to alienate potential community support. They have played a strong adversary role with local realtors who were trying to blockbust in the neighborhood. They organized regular Saturday morning picket lines outside the offices of local realtors and they initiated an anti-solicitation drive, urging residents to sign a statement that they were not going to be selling their homes. But mostly S.C.C. has focused on what can be considered "safe" issues: sponsoring Health and Home Improvement Fairs, providing services for senior citizens, helping to get an educational facility for retarded children into the community.

While S.C.C.'s first Congress was in progress, an estimated three to four hundred people
were picketing outside the hall. These people
had established a counter-organization, the
Common Counsel of Participating Organizations,
to oppose what S.C.C. appeared to stand for--
liberalism and integration. They also objected
to churches' providing financial support to
S.C.C., contending that such a distribution of
funds is an unwarranted mixing of church and
state interests.

The Common Counsel, like S.C.C., is an umbrella group, representing constituent organizations such as PTAs and civic groups. Their
name derives from the fact that "we counsel each
other" toward the goals of "quality education
and [raising] the economic standards of the
people."[10]

Common Counsel activities in 1971 and 1972
included: organizing demonstrations against
the court decision in Richmond, Virginia, which
ordered busing for the purpose of integrating
county schools; opposing sex education in local
schools and x-rated movies on television and in
the community; demonstrating their support for
the Chicago police; taking an active anti-
integration role in the local high school con-
troversy; and organizing opposition to the court
decision to place public housing units in their
neighborhood.

Many Common Counsel members express the
belief that there is a conspiracy operating to
undermine American society. When asked to
explain the conspiracy, one woman said:

> Well, I think it's all tied together into one big ball
> of wax. Education is one phase of it. . . . I see
> people trying to break the law and order arm of our
> country and what better way to overtake a country
> than to destroy the law and order arm? If there's
> nowhere for a person to go with your complaints, your
> grievances, or your protection, then that's a big
> step that the enemy's gained and I very definitely am
> aware that there is a conspiracy. It's just not
> logical to assume that all these things are happening
> by chance.

While the conspiracy is never precisely defined,
it clearly refers to the perceived threat of
Communist infiltration into American institutions.

In 1963, before either S.C.C. or the Common
Counsel existed, the Southwest Committee on
Peaceful Equality (SCOPE) was started.   Its
goals are limited.   In the words of a woman who
has long been a member: "We would like to see
the races live together in peace, and that's the
purpose."   As might be expected, the group has
little community appeal.

One woman active in S.C.C. describes SCOPE
as "a very do-good type of organization which
says, 'well, the best thing to do is integrate
the area and then our people won't be afraid
anymore and this would be just great.' And of
course people don't talk to these people. . . .
My feeling was like their program was kind of an
educational thing . . . and you could see they
weren't getting through to the people at all."
Yet a spokeswoman for SCOPE says that despite
the sparse attendance of only about ten to
twenty people at their monthly meetings, she
feels "just existing out here is something."

The neighborhoods in the westernmost part
of the Southwest Side are of more recent development than those in the eastern and central
areas.   While the other neighborhoods are losing
their white population, this area is gaining.
White population growth has been due in part to
the expansion of light industry in Clearing, but
it is primarily attributable to families leaving
racially-changing neighborhoods to the east and
settling here rather than in the suburbs.   One
informant, probably exaggerating, estimates
that as many as 75 percent of the present residents have moved from neighborhoods to the east.

Because these neighborhoods are not as old
as other parts of the Southwest Side and the
families have not lived there as long, there
appears to be less sentimental attachment to the
area.   There is less sense of community deriving
from shared past experiences and background.
People complain more about not knowing their

neighbors. They complain too about the "isola-
tionist mentality" of the residents.

> There's pride in your own little thirty feet or
> whatever it is. Beyond that, it's apathy. The thing
> about walking your dog at the school, but don't let
> him do it on my lawn. The typical mentality here. We
> keep our yard very clean, but we take our dog to the
> school where it's public property. To me, that
> typifies what the community feels. They're going to
> worry about their own thirty feet.

Another woman sums it up this way: "The only
thing that people in this neighborhood get en-
thused about is Little League."

Perhaps because there is less investment in
the community or perhaps because they have
already moved once, people here seem more ready
than other Southwest Siders to entertain the
possibility of moving to the suburbs. Often
settling here was an alternative to buying a
home in the suburbs. One woman explains: "We
did look in the suburbs but neither of us knows
the suburbs, you know. I get out in the suburbs
and I'm totally disoriented, don't know where I
am or anything. . . ." These families are already as far west as they can go and still
remain in the city, so when they think about
moving, by and large, they think about going to
the suburbs. Nonetheless, most of them are not
planning a move.

LeClair Courts, a public housing project,
is located in a northern corner of this area.
The Courts have been completed since 1950 and
are now occupied solely by black families.
While black families have lived in the area for
years, they have been confined to the housing
project and a few blocks of single-family homes
surrounding it. The white neighborhood can, in
most ways, ignore the black community since
segregation in housing is maintained. Black and
white children do come into contact at the local
high school where there are sporadic incidents
of racial conflict, but on the whole the likelihood of residential integration is not as
immediate to these residents as it is to their

neighbors in other parts of the Southwest Side.

Industry in this area has been responsible for a pollution problem that has been a constant source of irritation to the residents. The pollution has also served as a mechanism for organizing in the neighborhood. The Citizens Action Program (CAP) is a city-wide organization that started out as the Campaign Against Pollution. One of CAP's local chapters is located in the Garfield Ridge neighborhood.

The Midway Organization (TMO) is another local organization (with ties to CAP) that began with a platform that promised, among other things, to combat the odors and smoke generated by a local factory. TMO, which held its first community-wide meeting in 1971, was immediately popular, attracting almost 700 people to that first convention.

TMO was organized by a local parish priest aided by several other young priests who were training at the Industrial Areas Foundation, a school started by Saul Alinsky to train community organizers.[11] Some residents who are familiar with Alinsky's organization view it as "radical" and a few of the more conservative Southwest Siders, including some members of the Common Counsel, have opposed TMO on this basis. There is a feeling among the membership that politically conservative individuals would not join TMO, but the president claims the political spectrum of participants is broad: "We have a lot of liberals, some racists, a lot of middle-of-roaders."

Tactically, TMO's members focus on carrying out "actions," that is, demonstrations or confrontations for the purpose of drawing attention to a problem. Because of the desire to maximize media publicity and public attention, actions are generally carried out during the day. Consequently, women who do not have jobs outside the home are the ones most likely to be involved. It is generally agreed that women are the hard workers in the organization.

TMO operates in close cooperation with CAP.

Both groups were started by Alinsky organizers
and there is overlap in both leadership and membership. The two groups have worked together on
actions and fact-finding research such as un-
covering tax appraisals and the real owners of
buildings. In fact, all the organizations on
the Southwest Side that have been discussed here
conduct research, and learning how to use public
records to uncover necessary information is a
learning experience which members value.

Although TMO has strong support among community residents, it is not without opposition.
The Vittum Park Civic League, for example, was
organized about the same time as TMO by people
who did not agree with that organization's
liberal political perspective. Still, the basis
of the differences are not clear to all members.
One woman who belongs to the Civic League says,
"TMO is like a rival organization and why I
don't know . . . it just doesn't make any sense.
I know they're working for good causes and I
know we're working for good causes, so why fight
each other? I don't know why the people are so
uptight. They say they're Communist. . . ."

Other civic groups in the area have also
publicly opposed TMO and its activities. Envy
of TMO's success may play some part, but distrust of the group's liberal tendencies appears
to be the strongest motivation behind the
opposition. The conservativism of some residents borders on paranoia. The president of a
local civic league, speaking at one of its
public meetings, declared: "If a housewife gets
up and starts talking and she is spending an
excessive amount of time away from home at
meetings, start asking who's taking care of her
expenses."

Although the priest who organized TMO and
the priest who organized the block clubs to the
east have little in common other than their
affiliation with the Catholic Church, both exert
a powerful and similar impact on their followers. Strong devotion to each priest is
evident within his group. In one case, photo-

graphs of the priest are prominently displayed
in the homes of members; in the other, members
indicate they will only attend Mass if that
priest is celebrating it.   It may be that a
priest, whose status makes him both protective
of traditional values and sexually non-threat-
ening, is a particularly effective leader in a
community where women's participation in organizations constitutes something of an emergence
from a restrictive environment and conventional
behaviors.

The Midway Organization, the Southwest
Community Congress, and the Common Counsel of
Participating Organizations share a number of
characteristics. Each is an umbrella organization, that is, each is a large-scale organization composed of representatives from a number
of smaller neighborhood groups. These smaller
groups join a larger, more comprehensive organization in order more effectively to confront a
shared problem.

Such a structural development, according
to Suttles, results from the fact that "local
community organizations . . . are too small and
so lacking in stature that they cannot approach
the high administrative offices which now affect
them. . . . Furthermore, they can seldom claim a
broad enough constituency to rightfully represent the people in negotiations with administrative offices above that of the local
district."[12]

Consequently, we see

. . . the growth of large-scale community organizations. Often, but not necessarily, confederational
in form, these organizations expand their membership
to include a wide range of residents, develop a more
professional and high status leadership, and attempt
to speak to all issues concerning a contiguous area
of considerable size and certainly larger than the
defended neighborhood. . . .[13]

A second trait shared by these confederational organizations is their tactical approach. As indicated, these groups have adopted

a direct-action, sometimes militant, approach to issues. Suttles suggests that such a tactical direction can also be attributed to the impotence of small, orderly organizations. As a result, "many small, local, and traditional community organizations seem to have resorted to more militant tactics in bringing themselves to the attention of higher administrators."[14]

One last area of the Southwest Side is the northeast section, an area which, by any socio-economic measure, is considerably less well off than the others. The neighborhoods are noticeably more run down, stores are closed or dilapidated, and residents seem to put less effort into maintaining their homes in good condition. Despite the fact that many of the men living here, in Mayor Daley's neighborhood, hold city jobs, the average family income is less than the city-wide median.

The famous Chicago stockyards were located in this neighborhood until recently when they were phased out and finally closed down altogether. For years, the stockyards had provided jobs for unskilled immigrants settling in the area. One woman explains her neighborhood's history: "It originally started out to be a German community . . . they came in from Germany to serve the yards as butchers . . . and then with the German immigrants moving away, the Poles took over and now it looks like the Mexican-Americans are coming in. . . ." Now, with the stockyards closed, this source of jobs is not available to any group.

This area is all white and these residents are alone in claiming they are not terribly concerned about the possibility of blacks moving in. "They call this 'white man's island'," one woman said in explaining that people really do believe that the power of Mayor Daley will keep their neighborhood white. In that neighborhood, for example, is the only public housing project in the city with no black residents.

Still, the neighborhood is undergoing change in the makeup of its population.

Overall, the area is losing in numbers: between
1960 and 1970, the population decreased by about
11 percent. The new people moving in tend to be
either poor whites from Appalachia or Mexicans.
Some of the Catholic churches are still national
churches oriented toward a particular ethnic
group. One Polish church, for example, cele-
brates a Mass each Sunday in Polish and, for the
older people, confessions continue to be heard
in Polish. Such national churches, however, are
fading out and will probably die off with their
elderly parishioners.

In this neighborhood which is experiencing
out-migration, who are the people who remain?
They are people who like familiarity ("if I walk
down the street, anywhere I go, people know me")
and stability ("mostly, you like to stay, you
know, where you're brought up and raised").
They are also those who cannot afford to move,
the poor and the elderly. Many of the area residents are living in family homes already paid
for; they are not financially able to move out
and purchase a new house. Many of the men are
in low-paying jobs with no hope for advancement
in the future and they are now resigned to not
"making it." One woman speaks of her husband:
"Staying down here is like he's really never
succeeded, you know, like most everybody in his
age group has moved away from down here. And he
feels they've bettered themselves."

Despite, or perhaps because of, the serious
deprivations in this area, there are no active
community organizations like those found in
other areas. It may be that people are so busy
making ends meet that neither men nor women have
the time and energy to put into such groups. It
may also be that people here are still dependent
on and trusting of the local Democratic organization to provide solutions for community problems. Here there exist a strong allegiance to
the Democratic Party and few of the independent
stirrings that typify the other neighborhoods.

There may be another reason why the community organizations with their active women

participants have not caught on in this area: the women may not be so ready to move into a new extrafamilial role. Women here appear to live in closer harmony with the sex role patterns traditional in their ethnic groups, patterns in which women's behavior is fairly constricted.

The area is not, however, totally without sparks of community life. In past years, citizens have come together for brief periods of time over specific problems. Citizens for Bridgeport, for example, was organized "to keep black people out of the housing probject" and again for a short time to get a fence around a quarry which posed a hazard to neighborhood children. Once the goals were attained, the group quickly disbanded. Citizens for Bridgeport followed the historical pattern: "Community organizations arise to meet a particular issue; they address their complaints or demands to one or a few service organizations; and, with success or failure, they all, except possibly the leaders, lapse into relative obscurity."[15]

Other areas of the Southwest Side appear to be breaking out of this historical pattern: they are organizing around more than one issue; they are surviving over a period of years; and they are not lapsing into obscurity after one issue is resolved. They are groups with long-range political objectives which appear able to hold together a nucleus of people over time. In this northeast neighborhood, however, this is not happening. A few women from this area were included in the inactive part of the sample.

It becomes clear in looking at the neighborhoods of the Southwest Side that there are histories and problems unique to each of the geographical areas. Still, the people in the different neighborhoods have much in common. Despite the heterogeneity of ethnic background, there exists what is perceived by some as a common culture. "They're all people like myself," one woman explains. "They were raised the same way, the same sense of morals and right and wrong. . . . We're all the same." In trying to

gain community support for the high school boy-
cott, Father Lawlor appealed to a common culture: "Our culture is a shared culture. We all
identify with each other."[16] Some residents,
however, question to what extent there is a common culture that is more than just a shared
reaction of white residents to the threat of
black neighbors.

People in the community also share a reputation for provincialism and anti-progressivism
and they are aware of this. "Some people say
we're in our own little ghetto here," says one
block club activist.

> We're in an Irish ghetto . . . but if you feel at home
> with your own people, there's nothing wrong with that
> either. But some people will say you're in this type
> of ghetto, why don't you get out and see the rest of
> the world and all that. Well, I've been happy here.
> I don't particularly care to . . . I like it here.

Residents know their way of life is subject
to criticism from people outside the community.
But they do not accept the validity of the
criticism. They, after all, feel quite satis-
fied living with people who are like them.
"Here if I walk down the street, anywhere I go,
people know me," says one woman, pleased with
personal ties rather than anonymity. "I like
the people," says another, "there's always someone to turn to."

It is these personal ties and this sense of
shared culture and community which they feel are
being threatened. Everyone on the Southwest
Side faces, with varying levels of immediacy,
the possibility of moving. Few rule out this
possibility altogether. The security of knowing
one will spend the remainder of one's life in
the same house or in the same neighborhood is
absent for most families. The insecurity is due
to uncertainty about the extent and pace of
racial change in the neighborhoods. Residents
of the neighborhood bordering on the black community know they will be leaving soon; those in
the central area feel they will have to leave in

three to five years; and even those living in the neighborhoods farthest west suspect that the South Side will be all black to its western boundary in ten years unless there are major shifts in the city's social policies. Only some of the residents of the northeast area venture to say they will remain, and it is clear that their neighborhood's remaining white is tied to Mayor Daley's retaining political power.

There exists a kind of resignation about this likelihood of having to move. Yet the resignation is heavily laced with bitterness and, even more strongly, with sadness. "I just don't want to face it. My daughter says, you know you just don't move overnight, it's not gonna all happen in a month. I know that. I know it as sure as I'm sitting here. But maybe I'm hoping I'll die or something." These women anticipate moving with varying degrees of imminence. Yet most, regardless of whether they see a move coming soon or fear it in a more distant future, do not know where they will resettle when the time to move actually comes.

The suburbs are unattractive for a number of reasons, not the least of which is the reputed cost of living there. "It's so much more expensive to live. You need two cars. You have to pay taxes for water, extra for garbage collection, everything is an extra."

There are other reasons, too. A number of women express a fear of loneliness if they move away from family and friends.[17] One woman had already experienced such loneliness when she and her family moved from one Southwest Side neighborhood to another further west. Practically every morning for two years she took the bus to her mother's house in the old neighborhood. Even this method of countering loneliness would not be open to women who move to the suburbs where transportation is usually dependent on having a car.

However, something beyond the higher cost of living and the anticipated loneliness underlies the anxiety produced by the thought of a

move to the suburbs. There appears to be a fear
that family life, as these women know it and as
it reflects their values, will be threatened.
Again and again, this theme recurs. One woman
summarizes her fears:

> I look at the suburbs and I read in the paper how
> crime is bad out there and how they smoke pot and
> things like that and I say to myself, well, I got a
> large family and it's not like I just got older
> children that'll be leaving me in four or five years.
> I have younger children. And I figure my older ones,
> well, they're practically out of the wing of the
> mother, you might say, but the younger ones you got to
> kind of watch more. So I look at the suburbs and I
> wonder. . . . It seems like they let their children
> date younger out there, things that you don't do in
> the city where you can keep a closer watch on your
> children. This is what I find.

There is a belief that children may no
longer share their parents' values if the family
is transported to a suburban environment. There
is a fear that the children will no longer be so
readily under parental purview. It is more difficult to keep watch over your children when
everything is spread out geographically. Some
women also believe "you'll get all kinds of
people if we go to a suburb" and "you don't know
the kids, what they're like."

These city dwellers' anxieties about the
suburbs are striking in the extent to which they
parallel suburbanites' fears of the city. These
urban women are saying that they hear about high
crime rates, drug use, permissive sexual behavior, and all different kinds of people in the
suburbs. Why do they not recognize that all
these things exist in their city as well? In
part, such undesirable situations do not exist,
in extreme form at least, in their community;
and their community is the city to them. In
their community they know their neighbors and
they know what their children are doing. These
parents frequently express anxiety about their
children's growing away from them. A move to
the suburbs can only exacerbate such a fear.

If living in the city becomes untenable and
living in the suburbs is undesirable, what then
is left? For a few, some consideration is given
to moving beyond the suburbs to semi-rural
areas.   For most, there is an avoidance of
facing the concrete dimensions of the problem.

Women who are active in the community organizations seem even more unhappy about the
thought of leaving the neighborhood than do
their inactive neighbors. Leaving, after all,
constitutes an admission of defeat for them.
"I'm staying," says one woman active in the
block clubs. "My home is paid for and I have no
idea where I would go, where I would want to go.
So I would stay until it becomes too unbearable
for me, let me put it that way.   And it would
have to be pretty bad." Her insistence that she
will remain flies in the face of reality as her
neighbors, one after another, leave.

Another reason why active women may be
especially reluctant to face the possibility of
leaving their neighborhoods is that their organizational participation has provided them with
additional   strong   ties   to   their   community.
Women who might otherwise be at home and alone
during the day have found not only a new focus
for their concerns but also a new source of
friends.   Women from several of the community
groups speak of the neighbors they have met
through their involvement: "We've met people
that live on the next block that we didn't know
before." The organizations have been effective
in bringing people together and intensifying
social ties.

Some organizations, like TMO, appear to
have gone beyond intensifying social ties and
have actually taken on the characteristics of a
surrogate community.   People living in the
western neighborhoods served by TMO have not
lived there long; they did not grow up in their
neighborhood.   Because settlement is more recent, these families are less likely to have
relatives and old friends nearby.   In addition,
the neighborhood is not home for any particular

ethnic group or groups. Consequently, the
"natural" ties of shared ethnic origins, of
family roots, and of friendships of long dura-
tion that characterize the older working-class
neighborhoods are not present here. But a new
basis for solidarity is emerging: membership in
the community organization becomes the tie that
binds people together. One woman, active in
TMO, puts it this way: "At this point I would
feel bad [about moving]. A year ago, I wouldn't
have. But I've met so many interesting people,
interesting and interested, which we never
knew." Another woman has similar sentiments:
"If I had to move, I'd cry all the way there and
all the time I was out there because of my involvement in the community now and the people
I've met. You know, it's like one big happy
family." She goes on to add:

> I enjoy going to church on Sunday because I see these
> people and we have coffee afterwards. And no matter
> where you go, you go to the grocery store and you'll
> see one of them, and it's like you never went home,
> you keep seeing them. And there's so many of them and
> they're so great and they're just fun to be with and
> they're interesting to be with.

So in this area where traditional community
ties are weaker, attachment to the neighbors and
the neighborhood is expressed through organizational ties. The "one big, happy family" becomes not all the people who live nearby, nor
all the people who are Italian, nor all the
people who have been friends since childhood but
rather those from the neighborhood who share the
activities and concerns of the community organization.

This brief history of the Southwest Side of
Chicago shows the social context within which
the new community organizations have come into
existence. Clearly the neighborhoods on the
Southwest Side have been meeting crises they had
not previously had to confront. Paramount among
these crises has been racial change in the community, accompanied by the harassment tactics of
realtors, the anxieties of residents, and the

"defended neighborhood" responses. Although racial tensions have clearly been the major impetus to organizing, other crises--notably industrial pollution and poor school conditions--have emerged as well.

A crisis, as the Chinese symbol for that word indicates, presents both opportunity and danger. Certainly the dangers of these neighborhood crises have been evident; the fears and anxieties of both black and white families, the loss of a home and a secure future for families that feel they must move, and the increased disillusionment with city agencies and public officials are only a few of the most imminent dangers.

What is less evident is the opportunity aspect of these shared crises. The crises have called forth an organized and collective response which is fundamentally political in its assertion of power. For women, becoming active in these organizations means, in many cases, assuming a commitment to serious political roles. It is this which may provide an unanticipated and largely unrecognized opportunity for women to exercise skills, grow in self-confidence, and assume respected positions in the community. The remainder of this book will look at this new opportunity, at what has made some women respond to it, and at what the effects appear to be. First, the next chapter will briefly examine the daily lives and expectations of the women from the Southwest Side, and the extent to which the lives of these women correspond to the portrayal of working-class women in sociological literature.

[III]

Yesterday's Expectations, Today's Lives

> Well, I lived in Bridgeport all my life, and I went to parochial grammar school and high school, and I really never lived out of the community. And I worked, and got married, and have a daughter, and that's it.

One woman describes her life and its high points: school, work, marriage, a child. There is no embellishment of these ordinary events, no unusual touches which could give her life a peculiarly individual quality. In one sense, this woman is typical. Others provide descriptions of their lives that are similar to hers in their simplicity. Certainly the events that characterize her life are major in the lives of all the respondents and, indeed, in the lives of most women. Family and neighborhood constitute the core of life; a job may also be important, but generally less so.

Yet, despite the shared attachment to the basic social institutions of family, church, and community, there is variation in the lives of the women on the Southwest Side. For some, especially those who have become active in the assertive community organizations, there is far less routine than the woman quoted above appears to have in her life. One woman, active in her community organization and beyond, when asked to describe a typical day, laughs and responds:

63

I can't say I have a typical day. I have such
variety. Every day is different for me. I'll pick a
day out--all right, Monday. I get up, feed my kids
breakfast, straighten up the house, get dressed, and
I do volunteer work at the mental health center. I
come home and I feed the kids lunch and I do what I
can do between the time they leave for school, and
then I go to school. And I come home and I make
dinner, feed the family. The kids pick up the
kitchen. And if I'm lucky, I stay home [at night],
and if I'm not. . . .

A neighbor of hers, active in the same
group, describes a similarly varied routine:

I'll tell you a typical day in my life. I like to get
my work done in the morning. I like my house reason-
ably clean, so I kind of zip through everything in the
morning. Generally any activities I have in the
community are in the afternoon . . . if we have any
kind of activities to go to downtown or in the school.
Now the PTA, I'm active in that, I'm program chair-
man, I have a board meeting once a month. . . . I
indulge myself in my painting once in a while. . . .
It's kind of a mixture, a mixed bag of things. There
is no typical day. It's what comes up really.

Many of the respondents indicate an enthusiasm for new adventures which belies the
orientation to and security in routine which has
been said to characterize women of the working
class.[1] The daily lives of many of these women
would corroborate the findings of a recent
survey that the working-class woman

. . . is now less homebound than previously and more
active in the wider world of neighborhood and local
community. . . . She is more likely to be active now
in PTA, volunteer work, and in recreational groups.
Her circle of associations and friendships has been
widening, displacing her earlier tendency to confine
social contacts largely to relatives.[2]

So there are signs of change, indications
of expanding activities and interests. Yet, at
the same time, there is a desire to hold on to
the traditional and the familiar. There is a
wish to remain in the old neighborhood, a

concern that children will move away from parents' values, and a confusion about the changes in what their church teaches. Before looking at how some of these conflicts and wishes find expression in community activity, a brief portrait of the women and their backgrounds is in order.

All the women in the sample are white. They range in age from twenty-five to fifty-five, with a median age of thirty-nine. All but three--a widow and two who are separated from their husbands--were living with their husbands at the time of the interviews. All are mothers; about one-third have four or more children. These facts locate our respondents in a particular phase of the American female's life cycle. They are in the middle third of their lives, those years of young and middle adulthood that present demands in a variety of areas: as spouse, parent, citizen, and worker.

Most of the women (55 percent) have graduated from high school but had no further education. A few have not completed high school, and about one-third have some college or post-high school training, although only one woman is a college graduate. The education of the respondents' husbands presents a picture with more extremes: more than twice as many husbands have not completed high school (23 percent), but also more husbands have at least some college (43 percent).

Husbands' occupations are about evenly divided between blue-collar and white-collar jobs. Almost half the men are skilled laborers or city workers, such as policemen or firemen; about two-fifths are employed in sales, technical, or low-level white collar jobs; a few own their own small businesses; another few are unemployed. The median and modal income of these male workers in 1971 was $12,000. The mean family size is eight, but the median family size of five is probably a more accurate reflection of the average family.

The Southwest Side is a Catholic community:

90 percent of the respondents are Catholic, as are their husbands. In terms of ethnic background, there is more diversity. Almost three-fifths of the respondents are from unmixed backgrounds, that is, the nationality of both parents is the same. Most of the others, from mixed backgrounds, had no problem picking the ethnic group with which they identified more strongly. The final breakdown is: thirteen Irish; ten Polish; five German; three Italian; four from various other backgrounds; four who were "mixed" and unable to choose one; and one woman who would identify only as "American."

In a time when geographic mobility characterizes the American population, the women of the Southwest Side have led notably stable lives. Most of them have lived in the same area for their entire lives: 75 percent were born on the Southwest Side. Few, of course, live now in the same house in which they grew up. Marriage and children bring moves to new homes. The average length of residence in their present homes is twelve years for these families. The range in years of residence in the same house, from three to forty-four, largely reflects where the families are in their life cycles.

When moves from one house to another do occur, they are generally within the same community.[3] When asked where they had lived before moving to their present homes, all but three mentioned a neighborhood on the Southwest Side. Among those who leave the neighborhood upon marrying, a move back is not uncommon. "I was born and raised in this neighborhood," says one woman, "so was my husband. Then, when we got married, we moved to 52nd Street. We lived out there for four years; then we moved back."

Most of the women have never lived outside the city of Chicago. A few have, usually only for short periods. Most often this was during a time when their husbands (or fathers) were in the armed forces, and they lived with them at an out-of-town base. Having lived in the same community all their lives, most of the women remain geographically close to other members of their families. Almost four-fifths of the respondents' parents who are still alive are living on the Southwest Side. Other family members-- brothers, sisters, and grandparents--also live nearby.

Although family members are near, this fact is seldom mentioned by the women when they discuss why they wish to remain in their neighborhoods. Only a few make direct reference to the presence of their families. One says, in passing, "We wouldn't like leaving because our family is here." Another talks about moving but adds quickly that she would not leave "until all of my family has gone, because of the fact that my mother and dad are still here, my sister. . . . I would feel fine if I didn't have any of my family, but I don't think I could go and leave my family." Most, however, do not mention the presence of their families. There appears to be an assumption that parents will live nearby and, further, that they will go with their children should a move become necessary.

Despite their past stability, over one-quarter of the families anticipate a move in the foreseeable future. Almost invariably this is seen as an inevitable result of racial changes in the neighborhood. However, most of those who anticipate moving indicate they will stay on the Southwest Side and simply move further west; their intention is to continue living within the wider community. Only a very few say they will go to the suburbs, while a few more choose the North Side of Chicago or express uncertainty about where they will go.

While a majority of women are not yet planning a move, most will qualify their intentions of remaining in the immediate neighborhood. One plans to stay "until it becomes unbearable for me." Another is more explicit: "I'm gonna stay here until the event that I'm surrounded by black people. Then I would leave." All expect a move might be an eventuality.

Those who are not planning on moving were

asked where they would go if they had to move.
"I don't know" is the most frequent response,
followed by those who say they would stay on the
Southwest Side. A few select the suburbs, the
North Side of the city, or opt for getting out
of the Chicago area.

It is clear that the idea of moving means
changing houses and perhaps neighborhoods but
not, if it can be helped, leaving the community
altogether. Few can imagine themselves in the
suburbs, and even fewer are able to see themselves living outside the Chicago metropolitan
area. Respondents who are not anticipating a
move also experience a good deal of difficulty
in even imagining themselves living in another
neighborhood.

Despite the prevalence of long-time residence in the community, there is little visiting
back and forth among neighbors. One woman after
another said, "This is not a coffee-klatching
neighborhood." Privacy is highly valued, and
attempts at intimacy are viewed with some suspicion. Yet, as Fellman and Brandt also found in
their study of a working-class neighborhood outside Boston,[4] while frequent and intimate
socializing is neither practiced nor desired,
residents clearly value their neighbors. The
ethic of "minding your own business" is strong,
but also strong is the confidence that long-time
neighbors can be trusted and counted on in
crises.

Participation in church and school groups
is common for these women. Unlike the working-
class women in Rainwater's and Komarovsky's
studies who were found to join no clubs, only a
few of the Southwest Side women indicate a total
absence of organizational affiliation. However, the parents' group at school and the
women's club of the parish are the extent of
organizational participation for most of the women who are not active in an assertive community
organization. The women who are active in
assertive community organizations are just as
likely to be involved with church affairs and

more likely to be involved with school affairs
than their inactive neighbors. Many of the
active women participate in the traditional
civic group in their neighborhood as well as in
the assertive organization.

Other groups which find some affiliates in
the community are Boy Scouts, Little League, and
the YWCA. Some women, too, participate in
groups which reflect a concern particular to
them. One woman, for example, belongs to a
group made up of parents of retarded children;
another belongs to Al-Anon, a group for spouses
of alcoholics.

Organizational affiliation, then, while
not widespread in terms of either the number of
groups any one woman belongs to or the range of
groups represented, is certainly not absent from
this community. Some kind of affiliation with
the school and, especially, with the church,
seems to be important. It is within the church
and the school that basic values are taught and
reaffirmed. The strong bonds which exist among
these neighbors, despite minimal visiting and
social contact, are based on perceived similar-
ities in values and life style. The coming
together at church and school functions may provide the occasion for a reaffirmation of such
shared values and, in the absence of any other
mechanism for regular contact among neighbors,
may be especially important.

These bonds between neighbors, forged by a
similar life style and a set of shared values,
result in the belief that neighbors can be
trusted and counted upon in times of need. Such
bonds and sentiments of mutual confidence weaken
when a neighborhood begins to undergo racial
change. Fear, distrust, and suspicion replace
the older, more positive ties. "People over the
years you've given your house key to when you're
away and you always knew were there in case of
emergency, just all of a sudden, everybody iso-
lates and they don't believe all of a sudden."
This occurs even among those who have joined the
community organizations, as one woman explains:

"The people that were there at the block club, I felt, were sincere in saying they were not going to run, but the next thing you know you look out your front window and they are showing their house."

Most of these respondents, at some time in their lives, had a dream to "be" something. When asked what, as girls, they had wanted to do when they grew up, almost all were able to recall some goal they had. The traditional female occupations--teacher, nurse, social worker-- were the most popular girlhood ambitions, but a few had less conventional aspirations: journalist, veterinarian, artist. Only two or three have come even close to realizing their early desires. Yet there are few traces of bitterness evident. As Davis found in her study of blue-collar adolescent girls, desires are readily recognized as being discrepant with realistic expectations.[5]

Many of the women are able to articulate the decline of their aspirations. As young girls, they remember, they had goals; some even began college to realize their goals. But, over and over again the story is repeated, circumstances intervened: "I wanted to be a nurse. I still think about nursing, but other things, like falling in love and deciding to get married instead of following through with a career, just has its way of getting in there. . . ."

Sometimes the decision to abandon youthful dreams is made with more deliberation. The effect, though, is the same. "I really wanted to be a school teacher and I even started out to be one and I quit. I just went to teachers' college and decided I didn't like it, didn't want any part of it." One woman who recalls having no particular ambitions when she was young, wishes now she had: "When I got older I thought about a nurse, teacher, and then I never went to college. My parents wanted me to go on very badly, but I turned away from school completely and went out to work. . . . I want different for my children, especially if I have a girl."

For many, circumstances intervened before they had a chance to even begin approaching their goals. "I know I wanted to be a nurse. But it was pretty rough, because I was second from the oldest, and there were five of us so actually I really couldn't. I went to work to help out." Another speaks of the scholarship she was awarded: "I didn't take it, mostly because, with my father gone, we needed the . . . I wanted the money, so I went to work."

Some of the women have not really figured out what happened to their dreams, but wistfully acknowledge their decline. "Mostly I wanted to be an artist. I loved painting and that was one of my goals. I really enjoyed it. I paint every now and then, too . . . it was just sort of natural with me. . . . I think if I had gone on with that. . . ." Her voice trails off. That's clearly past.

Most of the women are not currently working at paying jobs outside the home. Only about one-fifth are employed, and half of these are part-time workers. Not surprisingly, women who are active in the assertive community organizations are less likely to be holding paying jobs than those who are not active. The income brought home by the working women is low. In 1971, 60 percent earned $4,000 or less, while the remaining 40 percent earned between $5,000 and $8,000. The jobs they hold are primarily clerical, although a few work at unskilled jobs, such as affixing price tags to drugstore merchandise, and a couple are in para-professional work, such as teaching kindergarten in the local Catholic school.

Still strong in this community is men's resistance to their wives' working. Almost half the women say their husbands are totally against their working. Another 25 percent see their husbands as ambivalent: while there are some aspects of their working that they feel their husbands like or would like--usually the financial increment--they know that the men would generally prefer them to be at home. Only two women have husbands who actively support their

working.   The remaining 25 percent feel their
husbands do not care one way or the other, but
simply believe that they should do whatever
makes them happy.

The reasons the men do not want their wives
to work are generally the traditional ones about
a wife's place being in the home and with the
children. Sometimes the minimal financial gain
in return for the woman's output of time and
energy is also mentioned, although this concern
appears to be expressed more often by the men
than by the women. "He won't allow it. He says
to me, what you have to pay out of taxes
wouldn't be worth it." Most of the women, at
the time of the interviews, did not feel they
had to work to make ends meet. Additional income might be helpful, but it was not essential.
Their husbands, while holding jobs which provide
minimal opportunities for enhancing feelings of
personal worth and success in the wider world,
continue to seek the feeling of self-respect
which derives from the fact that a man is
capable of supporting his wife and children by
his efforts alone. Indeed, as Sennett and Cobb
found,[6] the major gratification many working-
class men derive from their work is precisely
the realization that it allows them to provide
for their families. These wives, while often
wishing they had a job, are clearly sensitive to
their husbands' feelings in this area.

Strong opinions about women not working,
however, are not limited to husbands but are
held by many of the women themselves. "My husband doesn't believe in women working," says one
mother of two teen-agers. "He can afford to
believe this because policemen are getting a
good salary and we do what we can on it . . .
and I agree with him. Actually, I hated
working."

Not all women, however, are completely in
agreement with their husbands' decisions that
they not work. One woman poignantly expresses
her dissatisfactions:

I wish I did work. . . . [But] he feels that I, that a

woman, should be at home taking care of her family,
that a family suffers when the mother isn't there.
. . . I think a woman, sometimes, when she has a lot
of children, she needs a little, to know what being
away is like. . . . I feel that, even if I only worked
for a month out of a year, you know, just to get out
of the slump. . . . You get so you don't care how you
look. I mean, like you got to have like a different
little feeling inside of you that you're still, you
know, a woman, and not just a mother. I mean, you
gotta feel like you're still somebody. . . . But my
husband, he don't believe a woman should work if she
has a family. No. Because I suggested it a couple of
times and he just said, no. . . . The mother is the
one who keeps the morals of the house. She's the
moral keeper, he feels.

About half the women who are not working
say that sometimes, at least, they wish they
were. Still, the women go along with their husbands' wishes. "In order to keep peace, I
guess," says one. "Some men would make life
difficult." And some husbands do, in fact, make
life difficult when their wives attempt to take
on a job. "He never liked it," says one woman
who is now separated from her husband. "I think
his attitude is I should be home with the kids
and it's my full responsibility. . . . I had a
weekend job at a pizza place but he never liked
it. I had to quit, in fact, because he wouldn't
come home to take care of the kids."

All these women are or have been married
and most find it easy to discuss why they married and what they expected. For many, marriage
is the routine and unquestioned goal of a woman's life. These women, as Rainwater characterizes them, "have always known that their reason
for existence is to be wives and mothers."[7] One
respondent discusses such routine expectations
for marriage: "Well, when we got married, what
did we expect? Just to have a nice home, and a
family. We all knew that that was part of it,
especially if you were a Catholic." Although
all view marriage and motherhood as their major
life roles, one woman expresses this in particularly pragmatic terms: "I think having a family

gives women security, you know. You've always
got a job sort of thing as a mother."

"Security" is the single word most often
mentioned when the respondents discuss what
women expect from marriage. That single word
covers a range of concerns. "Women want security, mostly financial security," says one. "A
feeling of security, that they're going to be
cared for physically and emotionally," says
another. "Someone to depend on" is the way
another defines the security she needs.

Security may be what most of the women want
from marriage now, but in discussing their
earlier expectations a far more prevalent theme
is that of romantic fantasy:

> [Before marriage] women expect, as a rule, that they
> are going to have this fantastic man who is a great
> lover, and a more than adequate provider, and a do-
> it-yourselfer and just everything. And they're going
> to have two or three beautiful, lovely children, who
> are never going to do anything wrong. And be very
> satisfied with all this. They are going to stay home
> because you're supposed to stay home and everything
> will be lovely.

But, she adds, "after a few years, they are
very, very disillusioned." Another woman, too,
speaks of illusory hopes: "I think we live on
illusions about love and what things should be.
I think women want a romantic, idealistic,
never-ending honeymoon."

Only one woman cites companionship and the
sharing of interests, the aspects that middle-
class women often value, as something to be expected from marriage. At various times throughout the interview, however, it emerges that many
women would like to share experiences and
feelings with their husbands, but this is not
something they expect. As was the case with
their occupational goals, the discrepancy between desires and real expectations is by no
means obscure to these women.

While the respondents feel they know what
women expect from marriage, they are far less

certain about what men's expectations are. Several readily admit that they do not understand men. "I don't really know what men want out of marriage. I guess a woman wants to be taken care of mainly. Maybe some men want this, somebody to rely on and think they're the greatest in the world. It's hard to say about men. I don't understand them. They're very complicated to me."

Perhaps these women are unclear about what men want because they have trouble talking with and understanding their husbands, either because "he's not an understanding type guy" or because "there are times when he shuts me out and I can't talk to him. I have to wait until it wears off and then I go back to him." Komarovsky found the gulf between the sexes to be so wide that any empathic abilities were strained to the extreme.[8] While the gulf between these women and their husbands does not appear to be so wide, it nevertheless exists.

A woman who has been at home all day, especially if she has had minimal adult contact during that time, often feels the need to have the kind of detailed conversation that her husband finds boring.

. . . your husband comes home and you're hanging on every word he says. It's exciting for you to find out that someone came in late. It's stupid, but really not that much happens unless you're really involved and I think your family suffers a lot then, if you're so concerned you're running all day. . . . I'm kind of tied down 'cause I don't have a car and I can't afford a baby sitter.

Thus, many of these women indicate the existence of a problem similar to that observed by Sexton:[9] the man in the family is often the woman's major contact with the outside world. Consequently, when he says little the woman is not only deprived of communication with him but also of an elaborated relationship to the wider world.

Those women who feel they do have some

understanding of what men want from marriage are most likely to believe that a man marries because he seeks someone to take care of him. One woman responds immediately to the question: "Men want to be waited on hand and foot." But then, abashed, she backs off. "No, not really." More typical is the woman who says, "I think men have to have someone to look after them."

The belief that a man wants a wife and a home that will provide him with a retreat from the outside world is also expressed. "I think they want a kind of refuge from the rest of the world. That's it. When they walk in their home, the rest of the world can fall down."

Most of these women see their primary function in marriage as one of caring for and emotionally supporting their husbands. Because this is what they believe their men want from them, these women take such aspects of their role as wife quite seriously. "He's never missed a meal in 25 years. I was always here to get dinner." The women who are active in the community organizations go out of their way to stress the fact that no outside activities will take them away from their domestic responsibilities.

The traditional norm that a woman has primary responsibility for her family's care and well-being is strongly adhered to. At the same time, husbands appear willing to assume a certain share of domestic tasks. Virtually all the women say their husbands help with the care of the children, or did when the children were younger. This is generally in the realm of playing with the children, rather than feeding, washing, and dressing them. Most of the women also indicate that their husbands help with jobs around the house, although there are often specific limits placed around the kind of work men are expected to do. One woman who has been holding down a job to support the family since her husband was laid off from his job as a butcher says, "Yes, he'll do shopping for food but he's not ironing or cooking or nothing like that."

Caring for their children, along with meeting their husbands' needs, is viewed by the women as their major responsibility. Yet there emerged a somewhat reluctant recognition of the value to some mothers of sharing the task of child care with others.

In discussing the merits of child care centers, over half the women voiced support for them. "I think they're good," says one mother of ten.

> I think they really are good, especially for those very low income, both white and black. I think if they could basically get at it, those are the ones who need it . . and it would get the woman out, and she'd feel like a human being. . . . . I think the government should really put their efforts in that, in the inner city.

Even some women who are not very enthusiastic about such centers express qualified support for them: they might be good for those women who have to work and cannot afford baby sitters.

Only a few women are totally opposed to child care facilities, but they are vehement in their opposition: "I don't believe in them. I believe that this is the most important part of a child's life, when you're that little, and where they're going to get all their, you know. . . . They should have the mother there with them instead of dumping them off in some day care center." This woman goes on to add that she would never use one even if she had small children and had to work. "I would try and work nights or something like that, so I could be with my children. I would try all means before I would put mine in anything like that. I would object to it. I think it would be harming the child."

Many of the women who acknowledge a need for child care centers for other women stop short of saying they would use such facilities themselves. "I don't think I would send my children to 'em," says one woman who had earlier supported the idea of such centers. "I could go

full-time to work, because I have secretarial
courses, but my husband says no, and I agree
with him. He wants me home when the children
come home . . . and I can't see putting my
children in somebody else's care for eight or
nine hours a day. . . . It's not a home environment."

In the area of marriage and the family,
then, most of the respondents express fairly
traditional values. While their husbands may
provide some help around the house and while
they acknowledge the need for child care centers
under certain extenuating circumstances, there
is little overt questioning of the belief that
their primary role as adult women is to care for
their husbands and children. In exchange for
this, while they must give up girlhood aspirations to achieve and deep desires for emotional
intimacy, they receive security--a security
which not only provides for their basic material
needs, but also assures that as adult women they
will have an essential role to play in the lives
of others.

Living harmoniously and getting along with
people is seen as one of the most valuable
qualities a woman can possess. Concomitantly,
easily losing one's temper or otherwise being
discordant is seen as a negative, though not uncommon, quality.

This conclusion emerges from the results of
an attempt to probe the women's feelings about
themselves by asking them to name the things
they most like and dislike about themselves.
While they were free to mention as many things
as they wished, only one-third of the women mentioned three or more qualities. Most named only
one or two things in themselves which they
liked. Two women could not think of anything
about themselves which they found likeable.

The quality which was most frequently mentioned first as a positive trait is living
harmoniously with others; 40 percent mentioned
some variant of this. To be friendly, not to
lose your temper, to like people--in short, to

get along--is clearly a good quality for women
in this community to possess. Nothing else is
mentioned with anything approaching this fre-
quency. Positive intellectual traits ("I think
I'm smart"), "female" virtues (being kind or
quiet), and "androgynous" virtues (honesty, independence) are each chosen by a few women.

On the whole, the women are inclined to
like more things about themselves than they dislike. Almost three-fourths of the sample named
only one or two things about themselves that
they dislike. "Losing my temper," "exploding,"
or "screaming" are behaviors the women see in
themselves and do not like; one-third of the
respondents named such a trait first when asked
what they disliked about themselves. Another 20
percent chose something along the lines of being
too impetuous, too outspoken, or overly enthusiastic. These selections indicate that losing
control over oneself or being in some way im-
moderate is not acceptable, or is, at least,
something which must be checked. Over half the
women see such undesirable qualities in themselves. The only other selection of any substantial proportion relates to a kind of dissatisfaction with one's personality, for
example, being too nervous, or jealous, or not
sufficiently forceful. Almost one-third indicated such shortcomings in themselves.

Women who are very active in the assertive
community organizations are much more likely
than their inactive neighbors to see more qualities in themselves that they dislike. Almost
half of the very active women name three or more
qualities in themselves that they dislike, while
only two of the inactive women do so. This may
reflect a greater dissatisfaction with themselves and a greater restlessness which might
have helped propel these respondents into becoming involved in the first place. Or it may
be a result of the organizational activity. By
increasing the women's exposure to other people
and other situations, such activities may have
made them more self-conscious about themselves,
more aware of the weaknesses they might have in

comparison to others, and generally more self-critical.

The fact that being liked and getting along with others is so highly valued, while verbal outbursts, anger, and displays of emotion are viewed so negatively, provides an interesting backdrop against which to view the shifts which appear to be taking place in the lives of these women. Any substantial change in women's extra-familial and political roles will be forged from some conflict and may well result in even more intense conflict. This appears inevitable: a major shift in what a group does will invariably be upsetting to others who will be affected by that change. If the women of this community are experiencing pressures to assume an assertive extrafamilial role, on the one hand, and, on the other, they continue to cherish internal stan-dards which find conflict and discord unaccept-able, there can be little doubt that many will experience internal strain as they attempt to reconcile the conflicting demands being made of them.

With respect to religion, most of the women in the sample are practicing Catholics, although several mentioned that they are not as strict and conscientious in their practice as they used to be. The women who are active in community organizations tend to be more regular than the others with respect to churchgoing; all but two of the active women go to church each week while only 60 percent of the inactive women do so. Going to church, like participating in a commu-nity organization, constitutes both a social activity and a duty. It seems reasonable, then, that women active in one sphere are likely to be active in the other.

The two women activists who no longer go to church regularly represent a particular kind of perspective which is not uncommon in the commun-ity: the conservative view which resists "liberal" changes in general and integration in particular and believes the Church, by cooper-ating with the more moderate elements of the community, has "sold out." One woman, who is dedicated to keeping her neighborhood white and continues to consider herself a Catholic although she no longer participates in the activities of the Church, sets forth this position:

> As the sermons became political speeches I couldn't take it. I'd come home from Mass very upset, because they didn't have sermons in the real sense. . . . So I argued with the priests and they were very amused and they told me I was the only one that felt like that and Father [X] at that time was very active in civil rights marches and everything.

> You know, there's a certain order in civilization and I saw it all crumbling. . . . And when I saw this crumbling I really felt that this was evil taking over, to destroy all the beauty and the meaning in the Church. . . . I would question my older children, what did you learn in CCD [Sunday School] classes? We had a movie on integration. Oh, is that it? That's what you had in CCD, huh? So I didn't have them go anymore.

Another woman, herself a liberal with respect to integration, observes a similar process among her neighbors: "I find that many people who are very anti-Negro are now becoming anti-Catholic even though they are themselves Catholic. They feel the Church is pushing this on them, so they don't go to Church anymore. . . ." It is impossible to estimate how widespread such sentiment is. Where such feelings of antipathy toward the Catholic Church do exist, however, people continue to define themselves as Catholic. It is the Church that has left them, they feel, not they who have left the Church.

As indicated earlier, there is more diversity in this community along ethnic than along religious lines. Most families, however, are of European origin. There is a noticeable absence of Spanish-speaking as well as Jewish and black residents. Beyond this evident fact, ethnicity appears to be of little salience to most respondents. While almost half the respondents maintain some ethnic traditions, these are concentrated, by and large, in the areas of cooking ethnic dishes and maintaining holiday traditions. Often even these simple customs continue to be carried out primarily because the parents of the respondent or of her husband still enjoy the foods and the traditions. In discussing the customs they continue to observe, there is a noticeable casualness: "We do the blessing of the Easter baskets and occasionally we do the breaking of the bread on Christmas Eve, and some of the Polish cooking. And we use a few Polish slang words around here. . . ."

The casualness in the observation of traditions is matched by the absence of any strong commitment to the fostering of an ethnic identity. When asked "Do you think it is important to teach children anything about their ethnic heritage?" most women admit that it is not terribly important to them. One woman's response is fairly typical:

I think it's nice for children to know. I wouldn't say you have to pound it into them that they're this descent and that's the best descent there is. That I don't believe. Once they're born in America, they're Americans with this descent. And proud. Nothing to be ashamed of. You should be proud of that, but it doesn't matter what you are.

A few respondents express stronger sentiments, but in an unexpected direction. For them, a discussion of ethnic differences is neither casual nor unimportant; rather, it reflects an attitude that is un-American.

America, to me, is a conglomeration of people together and . . . our heritage is right here, and it's beautiful and the people that we know in the old country or from where we came, that's important too, but it's not first and foremost. And I think that people who are hung up on descent are not as hung up on being an American. . . .

The most widespread sentiment is that it is a nice thing if children are familiar with their heritage to some extent--it certainly is nothing to be ashamed of. Maintaining a few of the superficial ethnic customs is fine. But, on the other hand, neither is ethnic background something which should be emphasized. "You don't give children the impression that it makes them better than anybody else." An egalitarian principle appears to be in operation here, one that implies that people are all equally worthwhile and the differences among them are not significant. This is an interesting principle because its application, its "we" referent, is limited. It does not cross racial lines. Neither, as discussed in a later chapter, does it cross economic lines. Ethnic differences among these whites are relatively unimportant; but racial and social class differences are seen to be real and legitimate bases of differentiation.

What emerges in this discussion is a portrait of women whose lives are in transition. In the terms of Handel and Rainwater what is in evidence here is the movement from a "traditional working-class" life style to a "modern working-class" life style.[10] It is clear that many aspects of the traditional descriptions of working-class women no longer depict accurately the lives of these respondents. The women of the Southwest Side belong to more groups outside the family and participate more widely in the world beyond their homes than have working-class women in the past. Religious and ethnic attachments appear to have weakened. And the discrepancy between their ideals and the realities of their marriages and their lives appears to be more evident now than in the past.

Yet, in significant ways, their lives continue to fit a traditional pattern. Work outside the home is a major example: the husbands of the respondents--and many of the women themselves--continue to believe that mothers should not hold jobs outside the home. Geographic stability is another example: most of these women have lived on the Southwest Side all their lives. The geographic mobility characteristic of the middle class and of the less stable poor is absent.

In another sense, major in their lives,

these women are also in transition. Psychologically at least, most of the women are preparing to leave the community in which they have spent their lives. The crises in the community which are forcing responses in the form of organized community action appear to be accelerating a process of change which had already begun in the lives of these women.

[IV]

Who Joins? Political
Antecedents of Participation

There is discontent among the women of the
Southwest Side. It is from this discontent that
the new role of political activist has emerged.
Chapter II provided an overall view of the
situation in the community. This chapter will
look at the sources of discontent from the perspective of the women themselves. Participation
in assertive community organizations is a political act. Whatever nonpolitical reasons there
might be for some women's becoming active--and
such activism always results from a blending of
personal, structural, and political reasons--
there is, fundamentally, a political impetus behind such participation. There is an intention
to change the policies of institutions which
affect their lives, to change the direction
political leadership is giving, and ultimately
to shift the distribution of power. Not all of
this is articulated by every participant, but
implicitly such persuasions lie behind their
actions.

What are the immediate, tangible neighborhood concerns and circumstances which have moved
some women to take this political step and become activists? The women speak passionately
and concretely about what is wrong in their
neighborhoods and of how the structures of
official government--city agencies, the office
of the alderman, city hall--have not responded
to those problems. To understand these women's

assuming a political role it is important to understand both the roots of dissatisfaction and anger and the reasoning which helped direct that dissatisfaction toward political activism.

Overwhelmingly, what emerge as the major sources of discontent and dissatisfaction are, first, real or potential changes in the racial make-up of the neighborhoods and, secondly, the quality of the neighborhood schools. As might be expected, these two concerns tend to overlap.

Each woman was asked to name what she saw as the three most important problems facing her community. Over half the women gave one of their three choices to a racial issue. These choices reflect concern with the causes or effects of either real or potential change in the racial composition of the neighborhood. Despite the shared concern, there is great variation in the posed solutions. While all agree that the movement of black families into the Southwest Side poses a serious situation because of the intensity of white resistance, some deplore "the racism of the community" and "would like peaceful integration" while others want "to preserve the white race" and "prevent the colored from moving in." Most women, neither advocates of white supremacy nor avid supporters of integration, espouse a position somewhere in between: they would, they claim, accept a moderate amount of integration achieved at a gradual pace.

The "racial" problems mentioned often have little to do directly with either the white community residents or the black families that might move in. Often the "problem" is the way in which private and public agencies, such as real estate companies and the city school board, are acting in a racially tense situation. Realtor tactics are frequently mentioned and deplored.

I think that the real estate people are directly responsible for changing the community. In one area we took a survey, a mile square, and there were ninety-some realtors. They're very instrumental in the

deterioration of the community, the selling out of
the community. The people in this area have been
harassed by phone calls, get all kinds of literature.

Another woman includes the school board in
her indictment:

> I think it's inevitable, within five years the neigh-
> borhood will be all black. I'll tell you why: the
> school board and the real estate [companies] have
> done these things to the people. And as much as we've
> tried to voice our opinion in every matter and way,
> they won't admit it. We've done everything. . . .

Foreboding about public housing units,
scheduled to be erected in the community in the
near future, was also widespread and reflective
of the racial tensions. A series of suits and
counter-suits had held up action on a Federal
court judge's decision that all new public
housing units must be built in white neighborhoods at least one mile from the black ghetto.[1]
This would mean a substantial percentage of new
public housing units would be built in the
Southwest Side community. While construction
had not begun, sites were already designated.
Virtually all the residents of the community
have been adamant in their opposition to this
court decision. Some have formed a group to
fight the decision and, if that fails, to fight
the construction. There is little doubt that
public housing is equated with poor blacks
moving into the area. Whether the opposition to
public housing is based solely on racial grounds
or on economic grounds as well, reflecting an
aversion to having "poor people" as neighbors,
is a question explored further in Chapter VIII.
At least one woman claims a clash could be
avoided if "they would guarantee that they would
put white people [along with] black people in
their housing units--but they don't guarantee
that."

Even those respondents who view themselves
as more broad-minded than most of their neighbors are concerned about the effects on the community that will follow the construction of
public housing units. One woman, active in one

of the more moderate organizations, says:

> What frightens me is that people say, well, they're
> going to build them; there's no doubt about it.
> They're going to build them, but I'm not going to be
> here to see them. And I wonder, are they really in a
> position to be able to get up and go? . . . And it
> isn't even a black-white thing. As cruddy as some of
> the things look around here, people do try to keep
> them up, and they just have this fear, anybody who
> lives in a housing project is just not going to care.
> . . . And you can print all the pamphlets you want
> that say they're going to look for families where
> there's a father and people who will take care of
> their property and the people over here just look at
> you like you're crazy. Show me where!

Closely approximating racial issues as a
major source of concern is the state of the
neighborhood schools. Almost half the women
mention the public schools as one of the three
major problems facing the community. Overcrowding and the poor quality of the education
the children receive are the most frequent
specifications of this general problem.

Sometimes the expression of concern with
overcrowding in the schools only thinly veils
anti-black sentiments: such is the case where a
respondent supports proposed school boundary
changes that would all but eliminate black
children from that school. In a few cases, the
racial basis for discontent with the schools is
readily acknowledged by the respondent herself.
One mother says:

> Instead of pushing 200 black children into our public
> schools, if they only let it develop as the people
> moved in. . . . It would be a slow, gradual thing.
> The children would get to know each other. It
> wouldn't be this, this . . . and then this feeling,
> too, wouldn't prevail, that they were forced on us,
> they were forced on our schools.

Yet it is of note that even in areas
further west, where there are no black children
in the schools and no immediate likelihood that
there will be, schools are of major concern.
Complaints about the quality of their children's

education, in fact, were most likely to come from women in the neighborhoods more distant from the black community.

Indictment of schools often extends to Catholic as well as public schools. Catholic schools have traditionally been a refuge for white urban dwellers dissatisfied with public schools and, indeed, a majority of these women do have their children in Catholic schools. But, rapidly, the Catholic schools are either closing down for lack of funds and teachers, or raising tuition to levels beyond the means of working-class people. Consequently, Catholic schools are increasingly less able to provide a viable alternative to public schools for families like these.[2]

Other issues of some shared concern are pollution from local factories and the paucity of activities for children; 20 percent mention the former, 18 percent the latter. Pollution is most often a concern to women living in one of the westernmost neighborhoods where there is a factory that emits a notoriously foul-smelling smoke. The women expressing dissatisfaction with the lack of activities for children most often come from the old northeast section of the community, that area virtually devoid of community organizations where concern with gangs and vandalism is also high. These choices are pretty much localized, in contrast to racial and school concerns which are expressed by women throughout the community.

There are other problems mentioned: community apathy, drugs in the neighborhood, gangs, stores and businesses leaving the neighborhood, lack of health facilities, taxes, and property not being "kept up." The evidence suggests, however, that the general discontent in this community, among the active women at least, tends to center specifically around the inability or unwillingness of designated authorities to deal with the pressing problems caused by residential racial change and the deteriorating quality of education.

Concern with schools re-emerges when the

women respond to a question that asks what
issues they would select if they were going to
publicly protest on the following day. Almost
forty percent of the women mention school conditions. This issue receives more choices than
any other, and active and inactive women are
equally likely to make this selection. School
conditions are not only identified as a major
community problem and the major issue for public
demonstration but also emerge as the single
reason most often given by the women for con-
sidering a move to the suburbs.

This general picture of respondents' views
on the major problems facing the community is
found, upon examination, to mask differences
that emerge when the two groups of women--the
active and the inactive--are viewed separately.
Concern with racial issues and with schools is
considerably more widespread among the active
women than among their inactive neighbors.
Seventy percent of the active women select
racial issues as one of the three major problems
facing the community; less than one-third of the
inactive women make this choice. Equally
striking is the difference in the choice of
schools as a major problem area: 65 percent of
the active women make this choice while only 18
percent of the inactive do so. (See Table 1 for
a breakdown of the problems chosen by each
group.)

Inactive women spread their choices over
more problems; there is less focused concern.
They also have a tendency to select problems of
an idiosyncratic nature, such as the complaint
about the aging pastor of a local church or the
concern with a particular road that is not
paved. Such problems are undoubtedly of real
concern to the women identifying them, yet they
are not shared problems, not problems of concern
to any large segment of the community.

Another difference also becomes evident
upon closer examination: inactive women are
less likely to see community problems of any
kind. Only 20 percent of the inactive women

Table 1

Women Selecting Given Issue as a Community Problem,
by Activity Group[a]

Group	Racial Issues		Schools		Pollution		Youth's Activities and Gangs		Apathy		Stores Leaving		Drugs		Other	
	Per-cent	N	Per-cent	N	Per-cent	N	Per-cent	N	Per-cent	N	Per-cent	N	Per-cent	N	Per-cent	N
Active women	70	16	65	15	26	6	13	3	13	3	17	4	9	2	65	15
Inactive women	29	5	18	3	12	2	47	8	12	2	6	1	18	3	76	13

[a]Percentages are based on the number of women in the sample. Because each woman was able to select three problems, the numbers across total to more than the actual N of 23 for active women and 17 for inactive women.

could think of three problems facing the community; this compares to 83 percent for the active women.   Over half of the inactive women could name only two problems facing their community; eighteen percent could name only one problem; and one inactive woman could not think of a single problem in her neighborhood.   The inactive women appear less likely to identify a situation as problematic unless it immediately and directly affects them.   One woman, for example, who identified "more activities for the children" as "probably" a community problem went on to say, "but, see, this is another thing, my son doesn't have that problem.   If a kid wants to get active he can."

There are a few active women who could not think of a third problem facing the community. Interestingly, all four of these women had given one of their first two choices to a racial issue; two had given their second choice to a school problem.   In these cases it may be that not seeing an additional problem is less a result of not being aware of things in the community and more a result of the tendency among active women to focus their concern on the two major problems.

Activity in community organizations, at least in community organizations like those under investigation here,   appears to accompany not only a heightened sensitivity to local problems, but also a perception of those problems that is political and public in nature rather than personal.   It is of course to be expected that   the   community   organization   to   some extent will identify problems for its members. Women in the same organization often name the same problems;   they have, after all, shared work around those concerns.   It is, however, unlikely that the organization does all the defining   for   the   women.   A   minimal   prerequisite for joining an assertive community organization oriented toward change is the perception of a problem and a perspective that views that problem as both shared and amenable to resolution through group effort, that is, a political rather than a personal perspective.

There is something more involved here than
the ability among active women to readily see
problems in their neighborhoods. There is, as
indicated, a striking consensus on just what
those problems are: black-white relations in a
"changing neighborhood" and the quality of the
schools. These are the overriding concerns of
the more politically oriented respondents. And
these two concerns clearly touch on the most
intimate areas of the women's lives, their homes
and their children.

The kinds of schools their children are
attending and the impact of racial change on the
likelihood of their families' remaining in their
homes are not only pressing concerns, but, as a
number of the women point out, concerns
accompanied only recently by a sense of urgency.
As one woman puts it, "Until a couple of years
ago, there just wasn't any problems. Except the
garbage pickup, if it was late a day or so."
Yet, despite the recognition of these as recent
problems, the issues themselves do not far
remove the women from traditional female concerns. Homes and children continue to be the
objects of attention. The nontraditional aspect
of the role is the behavior that it calls for,
not the content of the concerns. This conti-
nuity with traditional concerns is important in
understanding the legitimation process involved
in the women's moving into a role that is new
and that calls for assertive behavior.

Something more than an awareness that their
personal problems are shared by others in the
community has moved these women into the arena
of participation. Coupled with their recognition of the problems is a perception that public
officials and agencies who should be responsible
are unwilling to address and resolve them.

In the course of discussing community
problems, respondents were asked if they felt
that their aldermen[3] were doing anything about
the problems they had identified. Among the
active women, two-thirds gave an unequivocally

negative response (see Table 2). Fewer than
one-fifth believed their alderman was actually
helping the community whose interests he was
elected to serve. The remaining 15 percent were
ambivalent or admitted they did not know enough
about what their alderman was doing to make a
judgment.

Table 2

Responses to: "Is your Alderman Helping
to Resolve These Problems?"
by Activity Group

Group	Yes		No		Don't Know		Total	
	Per-cent	N	Per-cent	N	Per-cent	N	Per-cent	N
Active women	19	4	67	14	15	3	101	21
Inactive women	29	5	18	3	53	9	100	17

Inactive women were slightly more likely to
have a positive opinion of their alderman, but
they were most likely to have no opinion at all.
While 29 percent of the inactives claimed their
alderman was doing something to meet the local
problems, over half admitted they did not know
what he was doing. Indeed, half of the inactive
women did not even know the name of their alderman. Often those who supported their alderman
offered uninformed or faint praise. One inactive woman who "thinks he's helping" could not
recall her alderman's name. Another who felt
her alderman's "door is always open" and "he
listens to us" could name only one problem
facing her community.

The active women have more facts informing
their judgments of their aldermen; they have had
contacts and discussions with them. They also
evidence more emotion and conviction in their
opinions. One, highly critical of her alderman,
was asked if he ever came to meetings of the
group to which she belongs. Her vehement reply:

He'd get killed, and he knows it. He really has been
a very mediocre alderman. Let's put it this way:
this is his second term; he had no problems. He just
came and went and he thought that was his job, and now
the problems are occurring, and we went down there a
couple of times and demanded things and we asked him
about the schools and all this, and he didn't even
know what we were talking about.

Another active woman, one of the few who
has a positive view of her alderman, says he
"has been very helpful. He really has. He
comes to our meetings and on Memorial Day he
came down to our Vietnam monument." This woman
is a member of a conservative organization whose
emphasis is on resisting change and preserving
things as they are in the community. The group
with which the critical woman works is pressing
for change in such areas as school boundaries,
tactics of real estate companies, and police
protection. She and her colleagues are de-
manding more of their alderman than that he
attend holiday rallies. Women in organizations
which are making greater demands on their aldermen might well be expected to find them less
responsive than those whose demands are less.

While attitudes toward aldermen are not
very favorable, attitudes toward the city
government are even more negative. Each respondent was asked if she thought the city government, on the whole, was concerned about her
neighborhood and the problems it is facing.
Only one active woman and four inactive women
answered affirmatively (see Table 3).

The most popular position, taken by 40 percent of the inactive and almost two-thirds of
the active women, is the negative one. The remaining women are uncertain. This political
cynicism is staggering: only one out of six of
these women believe that their elected city
government has any concern for them and their
community.

One woman angrily discusses the discrepancy she sees between her community's needs and
the city's responsiveness: "I don't think the

city cares about the community at all except
when it comes time to collect the taxes. I'm
surprised that they have garbage pickups. It
always amazes me when the garbage men come."

Table 3

Responses to: "Is the City Government Concerned
About the Problems in This Neighborhood?"
by Activity Group

Group	Yes		No		Don't Know		Total	
	Per-cent	N	Per-cent	N	Per-cent	N	Per-cent	N
Active women	6	1	65	11	29	5	100	17
Inactive women	27	4	40	6	33	5	100	15

Another woman attempts to elaborate on the
reasons for the city's lack of concern: "I
imagine [it's] because we haven't been very
vocal, so they just don't even consider us a
problem. We've never complained about anything
so, therefore, we have nothing to complain
about." Her sentiments are echoed by others:
"I think the city, or the machine, or whatever
you want to call it, for a long, long time
looked on the Southwest Side and said, oh, all
those city employees out there, we don't have to
worry about them. These are people who don't
ask for things, you see."

Regardless of political orientation or
activity level, there exists among these women a
strong sense that the city government is doing
little to meet their problems. Among the active
women, this feeling has grown into a firm
conviction that city officials care so little
about them and their problems that they must
begin forcefully to bring themselves to the
attention of those officials.

The sense of outrage at the lack of political leadership forthcoming from city officials
is fed by the fact that these residents believe

the existing governmental structure should be
responsible for alleviating local problems.
These women do not seek recourse through radical
restructuring of institutions. What emerges in
the course of the conversations is an acceptance
of the legitimacy of the government's authority
in making decisions about school integration,
expressway construction, and the control of pollution. Most respondents do not question this
legitimacy.[4] What they seek rather is a government more responsive to their wishes, a government that will make its decisions informed by
the needs and voices of the people.

These women are, in effect, recognizing
that the local political system as it presently
operates does not represent their interests and
does not seek out their opinions. But rather
than calling for the kind of major overhaul
which many believe would be necessary to assure
genuine democratic control of government policies, they ask only for more "informed" decisions on the part of those who now have power.
At this point in their political analysis there
is not a sense that their interests and those of
the city's major decision-makers are irrecon-
cilable.

Women of the working class, it has been
said, do not feel that they can exercise much
power over the course of events in the world
outside their homes.[5] Further, it is claimed,
they are not manipulative: they lack both confidence in their ability to influence people and
events and desire to do so.[6] While this may
hold true for some segments of the working-class
population, it is decidedly not an accurate description of women like those in the assertive
community organizations.

After identifying the single most serious
problem facing the community, respondents were
asked: "Do you feel people like you can do
anything about resolving that problem?" Among
the very active women, we see no evidence of the
feelings of powerlessness which have been attributed to women of the working class. This group
is overwhelmingly positive about their ability

to do something to resolve the specified problem: eighty-seven percent answer the question
affirmatively (see Table 4). Most of them not
only say they can do something but add that they
are in fact already working on the problem.
"People can do something by being involved, as
I am," says one active woman. "It doesn't take
any special talent. I think it just takes concern and interest."

Table 4

Responses to: "Can People Like You Do Anything
About Resolving That Problem,"
by Activity Group

Group	Yes		No		Don't Know		Total	
	Per-cent	N	Per-cent	N	Per-cent	N	Per-cent	N
Very active women	87	13	7	1	7	1	101	15
Somewhat active women	17	1	67	4	17	1	101	6
Inactive women	27	3	36	4	36	4	99	11

The remaining women, those who are somewhat
active and those who are inactive, are far less
confident about their ability to have any impact
on the problems they see. Over three-fourths of
these women either say no, they cannot do anything, or, revealing an almost equal lack of
confidence, say they do not know if they can do
anything to meet the problem. Table 4 shows the
first evidence of a theme which will re-emerge
frequently in the pages which follow: women who
are only somewhat active show themselves to be
considerably less affected by their participation than do members who are more active.

Unfortunately, such results do not tell us
whether the very active women had this strong

sense of efficacy prior to being involved or whether this feeling has developed as a product of their involvement. Women who are very involved in the activities of their community organization have had access to a good deal of research and information about what can be done and about what is, in fact, being done to meet neighborhood problems. All the active women knew of some group--usually the one to which they belonged--that was working on problems in the community. Such information and contact, at least during a period where there have been few organizational defeats, are likely to produce in participants the conviction that problems can be effectively confronted.

By contrast, 75 percent of the inactive women do not know of any organization that is working on the problems they have identified as serious. One who does not know of any group working on a problem is, understandably, less inclined to believe that problem can be resolved.

Regardless of whether the most active group felt efficacious prior to involvement or not, the point holds: this group of women does not exhibit feelings of powerlessness over external events, and it certainly does not exhibit any reluctance to engage in whatever manipulative actions may be necessary to produce change. Among the other women, however, the traditionally observed pattern--the feelings of powerlessness and uncertainty--persists.

What these responses suggest is that there is no longer (if there ever was) a single pattern of political awareness and concern typical of all working-class women. There are at least two such patterns. The women active in assertive community organizations emerge as better informed about community problems and more likely to see them as political issues, as more cynical about the willingness and ability of official public agencies and representatives to deal with those problems and, at the same time, as far more positive about their own ability to have an impact.

There is little doubt that participation in an assertive community organization is a politicizing experience in itself. The organization helps its participants see the political implications of their concerns, it moves them into situations of political confrontation and, as mentioned above, it arms them with information they would not otherwise possess.

Yet, the possibility must be recognized that the women who join and become active in assertive community organizations may have been more politically inclined all along. To explore this possibility, we asked the women to tell us something about how politically involved their parents were while they were growing up and how politically active they themselves had been prior to joining the organization.

On the whole, these women, both the active and the inactive, tend to come from families with no history of strong political inclinations. Their mothers did not provide models of politically involved women. Most say their mothers had little political interest beyond "doing their duty" as citizens, that is, voting. One woman, who is an exceptional case because she is very active in Republican party politics as well as in community groups, speaks of her mother in such terms.

> My mother's the type of woman, she's old country Irish, and the only time I can really remember her being interested was around election time. She'd start cussing a little. They'd be on TV and she'd start hollering. I can remember her showing more emotion when she was against something than when she was for it. . . . But she wasn't really active.

Several of the very active women indicate that their fathers were somewhat interested in politics. Fathers may have been a source of political influence for at least some of the active women. "That's all I ever heard in the house," says one. "Politics, politics. And I realize now it's a badge of honor that my father was a Republican in a neighborhood like that." This woman is definitely and proudly

following in the conservative direction set down
by her father.   But in the other cases, the
fathers' interest in politics was more vague,
often simply doing precinct work at election
time in order to keep their city jobs, and any
influence on the daughters has gone unrecognized
by them.

While there is some suggestion that their
fathers' political interests might have been a
factor in some of the very active women's becoming involved in politically oriented groups,
it appears that the women's political interests
are primarily a recent and independent development springing from immediate concerns.   Their
recounting of their own political activity supports such an interpretation: five years ago,
most of them say, they were involved either
minimally or not at all in any kind of political
activity or assertive community organization.

Although their parental families are not
recognized as a direct political influence,
their husbands, as it turns out, tend to share
the women's interests and concerns. Most of the
women who belong to assertive community organizations have husbands who are at least nominally
involved in those organizations as well.   This
suggests that the encouragement of husbands
might be a crucial factor in the wives' becoming
active. While that says nothing about direction
of political influence between the spouses, it
does imply that the active women live in a home
environment supportive of such an active orientation toward political issues.

At this point, a case can be made that even
prior to organizational affiliation these women
were politicized to the extent of feeling real
and focused anger over issues they defined as
political.   Beyond this, it is not yet clear
what other factors provided for some women the
impetus to become involved in an organization.
To better understand the dynamics of the process
involved in moving from a concerned but uninvolved to an active status, the active women
were asked to explain why and how they became
involved in their particular community organization.

In this context, half the women again talk about some specific problem facing them and their community that they felt had to be resolved. The same problems that emerged earlier--school conditions and neighborhood racial changes--are mentioned again, along with air pollution. Many women, then, define their mounting concern over a particular problem as the spark that moved them into action. This is hardly surprising. Yet only half the women cite this as their reason for participating. Most of the remainder say they joined the group in which they are active because someone in that group contacted them and asked them to join.

One very active woman explains the process by which she became involved, including both her desire to fight a particular neighborhood prob- lem and the fact that someone from the organiza- tion sought out her participation.

> I got involved because of the pollution from Union Carbide. . . . I've been ivolved with this [pol- lution] since I moved here when I got the first whiff. But I never had any organizational backing and really one voice doesn't do anything, 'cause I'd been calling there for all these years. You really need people. . . . [An organizer] called me . . . and said, remember when you were at that meeting and you spoke up about the odor? He said, would you like to come to a meeting tonight? We're having a meeting. And I said, fine, so I went, and that was the hooker. They got me started.

While the presence of a problem may be a necessary reason for one's becoming active, it is not in itself a sufficient reason. As the woman quoted above indicates, she lived with the problem for some time without acting to resolve it. As an individual, she did not have the re- sources or the power to confront the industry that was at fault. The element that moves a concerned person into a state of activity is the organizer. "I was kind of coerced," says one women who, although only somewhat active in the community organization, is quite active in her church and in Little League. "One of the

organizers came to see me because he had heard
that I was involved in many things in this
neighborhood. So at the time . . . I said,
well, I really can't do anything because I'm
much too busy, but I ended up more and more into
it. Because I really did believe in what they
were about." The organizer or leader brings
together people who share dissatisfactions but
have no structure through which to act on those
dissatisfactions; he or she coalesces the isolated individuals and provides them with the
structural prerequisites for action. "We were
all very happy to have a leader," says an active
block club member. "Everybody wanted to do
something, but nobody knew what to do. Father
Lawlor came along and he was a leader."

The importance that these respondents have
attached to being contacted reinforces
Rainwater's finding discussed earlier:
working-class women often would like to belong
to groups and would join if someone only asked
them. One woman, now very active, talks about
her feelings before joining the local organization: "I didn't know those people and you're
kind of shy, you don't want to go to these
meetings by yourself. I think it's nicer when
you know somebody and you can go in there with
somebody else instead of going in there yourself
cold." Later, after meeting one of the organizers at a friend's house, she joined the
group.

The need for friendly contacts to welcome
people into new social situations holds true for
most people, but the fact that voluntary associations are fewer in working-class neighborhoods
than in middle-class neighborhoods means that
working-class women will be less likely to be
part of a social network that includes organizationally active people. Thus, the structural
links that can connect community concerns and
dissatisfactions to political action have been
absent for these women. The community organizations themselves are, as we have seen, a recent
phenomenon.

The organizer has clearly been essential

for moving people into an organization and will continue to be important in determining the direction of an organization's future. Partici- pants in the assertive community organizations may feel burned out after they experience a defeat. Or, if they have not begun to take a broader perspective, they may withdraw after a partial or single issue victory with a faith in the responsiveness of the political system-- only to later face the need to reorganize when a new issue appears. It is also likely that cor- porate and city officials will attempt to defuse such an organization by offering minimal reforms and trying to co-opt key leaders. On the other hand, the community organizations may broaden the scope of their concerns and the base of their constituency and become a powerful force with which existing political organizations must seriously reckon. The future direction, to a great extent, hinges on the political orienta- tion and effectiveness of leaders and orga- nizers. An extensive analysis of the organizers and their role is not part of this study, but the indicators attesting to their importance are clear.

This chapter has shown the political ante- cedents of women's participation in assertive community organizations. The women who have be- come active are those who see serious problems in their neighborhoods, problems which affect all residents and which can only be resolved by collective action. In this community, they have been primarily, although not exclusively, prob- lems revolving around racial change and poor neighborhood schools. The activists do not feel that the responsible public officials are dealing with, or even concerned about, these problems. Accompanying the lack of faith in public officials' willingness to handle the problems is a belief, on the part of the very active women at least, that they themselves are capable of doing something to resolve them.

While all these qualities distinguish the active women from their inactive neighbors, it is not certain to what extent they are conse-

quent to participation in the assertive community organizations. The women, however, do not
come from political backgrounds, although there
is a suggestion in some cases that fathers may
have had some influence. Their participation in
assertive community orgnizations is their first
involvement in political organizations. Notably, in all of the activists' present families
there is at least tacit approval of their work
from their husbands.

Retrospectively, active women claim to
have joined the group to fight a particular
neighborhood problem. Almost as often, they say
they joined because someone from the group contacted them and encouraged them to do so. The
impression left is that political concerns by
themselves are not likely to lead a woman to
join a group and become politically active; contact with and encouragement from someone in the
group is the next necessary step.

Acknowledging the impact of contact with
someone from the group raises the question of
what other variables, not explictly political
and of which the respondents may not be particularly aware, are influencing the process by
which some women become active and others do
not. This question is addressed in Chapter V.

[V]

Who Joins? Psychological and Structural Antecedents

Clearly there are differences in perceptions of problems and in feelings of efficacy between the active women and the inactive women. While such differences may account for some women's becoming involved and others not, they do not appear to tell the whole story. Indeed, they may be effect as much as cause. The importance the women themselves have placed on being contacted by someone in the group suggests that a further exploration of variables in the respondents' social networks may tell something more about what precedes activity.

There are, as well, obvious grounds for anticipating that a woman's feelings about her neighborhood and herself may have some effect on whether or not she chooses to become active. And, finally, the other roles a woman is called upon to play and the extent to which these leave her with sufficient time to assume an altogether new and potentially demanding role is a factor to be considered.

Suttles argues that mothers have a considerable investment "in the defense of their neighborhoods" and also, for reasons relating to the protection of themselves and their children, have a "clear view of the neighborhood's internal structure."[1] Such knowledge of and investment in their neighborhoods, he claims, result from the confinement to the immediate area and constant attention to their children's well-being which characterize the mothers of young children. While this would seem to make mothers natural protectors of their neighborhoods, it has not always been so. Mothers of small children may protect their own homes, but they have not traditionally played a major role in making decisions about their communities. The community activists of the Southwest Side are all mothers, but the most active women characteristically do not have young children. Just the opposite is the case: the very active women are considerably less likely than the other women to have small children who are at home during the day. Only 19 percent of the very active women have children of pre-school age; in contrast, 50 percent of the somewhat active women and 60 percent of the inactive women have pre-schoolers.

There is another aspect of the life situation of the active women which has implications for their assuming a new role: they do not hold paying jobs outside the home. Only one active woman and one somewhat active woman have jobs, while, in contrast, 40 percent of the inactive women work at paying jobs outside the home.

The demands of these two roles--preschooler's mother and paid worker--would appear to (and apparently do) impose constraints on a woman's ability to participate extensively in community activities. Indeed, when these two characteristics are looked at together, we see that a full 75 percent of the very active women have neither a job nor children of pre-school age. In contrast, only one-third of the somewhat active women and 13 percent of the inactive women presently have neither of these role demands (see Table 5).

Clearly, the women who are most active are those who are not meeting the demands imposed by a job or small children. Over half of the women in this group are over forty years of age, further suggesting that participation in assertive community organizations tends to be a role

assumed by women who have moved out of that
stage of their life cycle where child-bearing
and child-rearing make heavy demands on their
time and energy and, at the same time, have not
assumed a role in the labor market.   Most of
them have entered or are close to entering what
Pauline Bart refers to as "the empty nest" stage
of their lives.[2] Their children are gone, or
at least are away from home during the day.   As
women whose lives have previously focused around
their children, they find themselves experiencing the loss of their most meaningful role.
So they are finding for themselves a new role, a
new space into which they can expand their
energies.[3]

Table 5

Women Having: No Pre-School Children; No Paying Job;
and Neither, by Activity Group

Group	No Pre-School Children		No Paying Job		Neither Pre-School Children Nor Paying Job	
	Per-cent	N	Per-cent	N	Per-cent	N
Very active women	81	13	94	15	75	12
Somewhat active women	50	3	83	5	33	2
Inactive women	40	6	60	9	13	2

The respondents, in discussing the general
question of who gets involved in community
activities, will often say, "those women who
have more time." The fact that the very active
women do not have jobs or children at home lends
support to such a generalization.   Yet this

answer is never given by any particular woman as the reason for her own participation. Time appears to be a necessary, but by no means sufficient, cause for a woman's becoming involved. Space in one's life for new activities does not determine the nature of those new activities. And there are some among the inactive and the less active women who have neither small children nor paying jobs. Precisely, the question to be answered is: What makes some women who have space in their lives for a new role and who are angry over what they see happening in their neighborhoods respond to the overtures of a group organizer and become politically active?

Initially, this question was explored in the context of two expectations held prior to the investigation. One hypothesis was that women who become active are likely to be those who are in some way more attached to their neighborhood and, consequently, more prepared to do combat with anything that threatens that neighborhood. A second hypothesis was that some women may have developed a particularly acute awareness about the ways in which they are oppressed--along sex, class, or ethnic lines-- and may have responded to that awareness by asserting themselves and making demands which speak to their own interests. Both of these hypotheses will be examined.

Any exploration of the women's attachment to their neighborhoods must begin with the basic fact that the organizations in which the active women participate are community based. They address themselves to problems which threaten the women, their families, or their way of life in their own immediate neighborhoods. This fact led to the expectation that women with particularly strong attachments to their neighborhoods might be the ones who become involved in the assertive community organizations. A woman who has lived all her life in one community and, consequently, has strong family or ethnic ties to that community might react with an "instinct" to fight and preserve her neighborhood and her

way of life if she sees that neighborhood being
threatened.

This hypothesis was tested by looking at
four variables which measure different facets of
community attachment: 1) length of residence in
the immediate neighborhood; 2) presence of other
family members in the neighborhood; 3) plans to
move; and 4) feelings about leaving the neighborhood.   In addition, respondents were encouraged to talk freely about their neighborhoods and what they like or dislike about them.

1) If longevity in a neighborhood indicates
attachment, such ties are fairly strong among
both the active and the inactive women. Most of
the women, as indicated earlier, were born and
raised on the Southwest Side. In addition, one-
third of the respondents have lived twenty or
more years of their lives in the immediate
neighborhood where they live now (see Table 6,
Column 1).

Occasionally, a woman moved out when she
was first married and later moved back into the
old neighborhood with her family when they were
ready to purchase a house. "I lived in the
house where I grew up until I got married, and
then I moved. And then when it was time for the
kids to go to school, we decided to come back
here so the kids could go to St. Nick's."

The inactive women have a slight edge in
length of residence, while the somewhat active
women, compared to both the other groups, are
relative newcomers to their neighborhoods. The
numbers are small and no distinctions are made
among respondents of different ages. Nevertheless, these figures clearly show that active
women have not lived longer in their neighborhoods than have inactive women.

2) There is a tendency for respondents to
have other family members living in the same
neighborhood. This is not unexpected as the
literature on working-class families consistently shows that elements of the extended
family pattern continue to persist in working-

class neighborhoods.[4] Interestingly, however, this pattern is considerably more pronounced for the inactive women, with 82 percent having relatives nearby. Only half of the somewhat active women and less than two-fifths of the very active women have other family members living so close by (see Table 6, Column 2).

Table 6

Women Possessing Selected Characteristics,
by Activity Group

Group	[1]20 or More Years in Neighborhood		[2]Other Family in the Neighborhood		[3]Plans to Stay		[4]Would Feel Bad About Moving	
	Per-cent	N	Per-cent	N	Per-cent	N	Per-cent	N
Very active women	31	5	38	6	88	14	57	8
Somewhat active women	17	1	50	3	66	4	50	3
Inactive women	40	6	82	11	60	9	38	5

If length of residence in a neighborhood and the proximity of other family members are measures of community attachment, it would be, somewhat surprisingly, the inactive women who emerge as most attached to their neighborhoods. These two variables, however, do not tell the entire story.

3) Despite the fact that they do not as often have family members nearby and are not likely to have lived as long in their present neighborhoods, the active women voice a stronger commitment to those neighborhoods. Eighty-eight percent of the very active women have no

plans to move from where they now live. This drops to two-thirds for the somewhat active women and 60 percent of the inactive women (see Table 6, Column 3). The active women are most committed to staying in their neighborhoods. But only a minority in any of the three groups has made any actual plans to move. As we noted earlier, however, virtually all respondents have the expectation that, at some future point, they might well have to move against their will.

> I would have liked to have stayed in this house, first of all because it's child proof, great for raising kids. The neighborhood was nice, because like I said, I knew a lot of people and the kids had a lot of friends. . . . I will feel bad. My husband, I think, will feel worse because he was raised and grew up around here. I would have liked to have stayed. . . .

This woman has made no plans to move and does not know where she will move when the time comes. Yet, she talks as if she has already left the neighborhood.

4) Finally, when asked how they would feel if they did have to leave their neighborhoods, it is the very active women who are most likely to indicate that they would feel bad about leaving: 57 percent say this (see Table 6, Column 4). The less active women are not far behind in feeling unhappy at the thought of leaving (50 percent), but those who are inactive are not so likely to say they would feel bad (38 percent). Most of the inactive women express ambivalence: they would feel some unhappiness at the thought of leaving, but they also have some desire to live in another neighborhood.

There appears, then, to be some indication that the active women, while not necessarily longer residents, have stronger positive feelings about their neighborhoods. Again, the causal direction is not clear; much of this attachment to the neighborhood likely has come about as a result of activity in the community organization. The close bonds between neighbors who share participation in an organization are described by one active woman:

We have gotten very active and we know a lot of people
who think as we do and we've formed kind of a community within a community . . . like a small town kind
of a thing. You need anything, you don't hesitate to
call one of these people.

Such bonds can be expected to make the
active women feel unhappy about leaving. The
bonds, however, are not with family members but
with neighbors who share a perspective and a set
of concerns. Getting to know such neighbors, a
number of women observe, has made their neighborhoods more desirable places in which to live.

The inactive women emerge as most attached
to their neighborhoods in a concrete sense--they
have been there longer and their family roots
are there; but the very active women express the
stronger emotional attachments--they like their
neighborhoods and their neighbors more and they
wish to continue living where they are. Attachment to a neighborhood appears to have at least
two dimensions. One dimension consists of the
attachments of time and family which may not include liking the neighborhood or the neighbors
very much. The other dimension consists of
positive sentiments toward the neighborhood and
its residents which may exist independent of the
attachments of time and family. It is this
latter pattern which more frequently accom-
panies activity in groups that are speaking to
community needs. Active women are more attached
to their neighborhoods, but not altogether in
the expected ways.

A second expectation was that women who
become active will be those who feel themselves
to be members of a group that is in some way
being maltreated or kept in a subordinate position by the wider society. Feelings of oppression might be experienced in a number of ways:
respondents might feel themselves discriminated
against as members of the working class, as members of certain ethnic groups, or as women.

The class and ethnic aspects of this
hypothesis derive primarily from recent works
which suggest that "white ethnics" of the

working class or lower middle class are feeling
passed over by governments, corporations, foundations, and others who wield power and make
decisions in this country and, at the same time,
are being blamed as the perpetrators of racist
and anti-progressive sentiments.[5]   Individuals
who have arrived at such a perception might well
be moved to an angry and aggressive reaction
which could take the form of participation in
politically oriented, assertive community organizations.

     To probe for feelings along this line, re-
spondents were first asked to designate the
social class to which they feel they belong.
The question was general, "To what social class
would you say you and your family belong?" with
no suggested categories.   About 90 percent of
the respondents answered middle class; only
about 10 percent identified themselves as
working class. This tendency to identify themselves as middle class likely derives from the
fact that ordinary people have a way of determining what is middle class that is quite different from the meanings sociologists attach to
that term.   One woman, for example, labels her
neighborhood middle class "because there aren't
any real rich people around here and there
aren't any real poor either."   As another says,
"We're in the middle."

     This tendency among what sociologists
call the working class to describe themselves
as middle class because they are "average" or
"in the middle" has been observed by others as
well,[6] and is a tendency important in its implications. The term "middle class" clearly means
something different to sociologists and to
working-class people. The claim that working-
class people lack class consciousness because
they do not refer to themselves as working class
but rather as middle class is questionable. The
distinction between "people like us" and other,
"rich people" is clear to these respondents, despite the fact that the labels they attach to
the class groupings differ from those of the
sociologist.

Respondents were then asked if they believe people in the class they had identified for themselves are treated unfairly in American society. As Table 7 shows, an overwhelming 92 percent of the very active women expressed the belief that people in their social class are indeed treated unfairly. A sizable majority of women in the other two groups feel this way as well.

Table 7

Responses to: "Are People in your Social Class Treated Unfairly?" by Activity Group

Group	Yes		No		Total	
	Per-cent	N	Per-cent	N	Per-cent	N
Very active women	92	11	8	1	100	12
Somewhat active women	67	4	33	2	100	6
Inactive women	73	11	27	4	100	15

The most frequently mentioned source of unfair treatment is the system of taxation. "Rich people always get out of paying taxes, 'cause they know the ways of getting around paying the taxes," explains one woman. "And the poor people on ADC [Aid to Dependent Children] don't have any money to pay, being that they're poor they don't have no money, so they can't. The middle class gets stuck with all the taxes." Again and again, an almost identical analysis of the tax structure is given by the respondents, both active and inactive. Almost two-thirds of those who feel that people in their social class are treated unfairly mention taxes as a major source of that inequity. Again, while this

belief is stronger among active women, a majority of the inactives who see class inequities
also cite taxes as a major source of those inequities.   It is striking the extent to which
the same story is repeated; the belief that they
are unfairly taxed is pervasive among members of
this group.

While taxes are the single most frequently
mentioned source of injustice, most women can
think of additional ways in which people like
them are treated unfairly.   Inadequate health
facilities are mentioned:

. . . medicine-wise, the poor people, although
they're certainly not taken care of adequately, are
taken care of by clinics. Your middle-class person
will not go to a clinic. And the rich people can well
afford the prices that the doctors are charging. And
oftentimes too the doctors will take poor people and
not charge them, but your middle-class people are
stuck with rich people's prices. . . .

As well, the women argue, they are made to
carry a disproportionate share of society's
burdens, such as experimenting with integration
plans or providing manpower for Vietnam, and
they are not provided with free or low-cost services such as children's activities and special
education programs.   "Not enough is made available by the government," says one woman who has
seven children and is separated from her
husband.   "Things are not made easy, that's for
damn sure.   You have to fight for every . . .
like, I never knew that welfare is a constitutional right, until this woman that I talked to
last week told me."   These observations, often
accompanied by a comment indicating that the
respondent is only recently becoming aware of
such injustices, suggest both a growing disaffection with the political and social structures
along class lines and an increased ability to
articulate the elements which contribute to that
disaffection.

A minority claim that people in their class
are not treated unfairly.   Many of these base
that belief on the fact that everyone is

deprived in some way and thus deprivation itself is equitable. "You have to work hard for what you want, but everybody does," and further, "You have to have a dream and want for something." Struggle is not unfair, but an expected part of life.

Feelings of oppression or a sense of unfair treatment along class lines are strongly held. Despite the fact that these women neither spontaneously describe themselves as "working class" nor spontaneously discuss the injustices they experience in social class terms, they do see systematic inequities which derive from economic factors: people in different income brackets are treated in different ways and have differential access to the good things of the society.

It has been said that the emergence of "ethnic consciousness" in the early 1970s, largely following the pattern of black consciousness of the 1960s in terms of emphasis on cultural pride and gaining control over community resources and decisions, has made white working-class ethnics more aware of the ways in which the American dream is no longer working for them. The upsurge in protest and organization in white ethnic neighborhoods is increasingly evident. The extent to which ethnic consciousness and, specifically, ethnic-based feelings of oppression or discrimination, feed into this process, however, is not clear.

Respondents were asked their nationality background and then asked if they felt people of their ethnic group are treated unfairly in any way in American society. Overwhelmingly, these women respond in the negative. Only four women, all of Polish descent, believe that members of their ethnic group are treated unfairly; primarily it is the contemporary cultural stereotyping of Polish people as "dumb Polacks" that they resent. Two of these women are very active in community organizations; the other two are not at all involved. Barring this exception, the women do not feel discrimination directed at them as members of a particular ethnic group.

Most of the women live in neighborhoods which are ethnically, if not racially, hetero-geneous. They have little difficulty seeing that their neighbors, of different ethnic back-grounds but of the same social class, live much as they do and suffer much the same hardships that they suffer. There is little experience or awareness of ethnically-based discrimination. Most women will speak of such discrimination as something in the past, something that existed once, but that no longer affects them. It also seems that racial awareness is so intense in this community that distinctions of race become the overriding ones and, consequently, ethnic distinctions within the white community break down.

Finally, feelings of being oppressed, ignored, or otherwise treated as less than equal citizens because of their sex were also ex-plored. Has exposure to the discussions within the feminist movement which have focused so much attention on the inequities experienced by women made an impact on any of the respondents? Do they see ways in which they, as women, are treated unfairly either in personal relation-ships or by society in general? If such feelings had developed, might not those women experiencing them be the ones most ready to join assertive groups? They would be the ones re-sisting constraints on their behavior and de-manding to be heard.

With these expectations in mind, each woman was asked if she ever felt personally oppressed or kept down in any way. These women, gener-ally, do not (see Table 8). "No, I don't really think so," says one woman who is somewhat active. "I think if I want to do something, I'm going to go ahead and do it anyway. From my husband, no, and I can't think of anybody else who would really oppress me." Another woman, who is inactive, responds in terms of her race and economic position:

I can go anywhere and get a job, I think. I don't think anyone because of my color or anything would hold me back. And if I have enough money to go out

and buy a dress, I can go out and buy a dress. I
don't feel oppressed or underprivileged.

Table 8

Responses to: "Do You Ever Think of Yourself As
Oppressed?" by Activity Group

Group	Yes		No		Total	
	Per-cent	N	Per-cent	N	Per-cent	N
Very active women	50	7	50	7	100	14
Somewhat active women	33	2	67	4	100	6
Inactive women	38	5	62	8	100	13

As Table 8 shows, there is a tendency for
the very active women to be more likely than the
others to think of themselves as oppressed,
although only half do so. Many of those who
give an affirmative response relate the oppression they feel to the problems they are confronting through the community orgnizations.
"[I feel oppressed] just in the things they make
you do with your taxes and that," says one. And
another active woman responds, "Well, I do feel
sometimes the things we're trying to do in the
community, we're held down by the system."

As these quotations indicate, few of the
women who acknowledge a sense of oppression see
it as deriving specifically from their sexual
status. The injustices they experience are not
felt to be primarily based on the fact that they
are female. The major exception to this is one
inactive woman who is separated from her husband
and has had direct contact with activists within
the feminist movement. When asked if she feels
oppressed she responds:

Yes, definitely. . . . If my kids get sick, I don't
know what I'm gonna do. I can't get a decent job

because I'm a woman, you know; I'm not gonna get the
pay that a man can get. That makes me have to depend
on a man that is undependable.

Several other women who speak of being
sometimes overwhelmed by household demands do so
in a way which trivializes their concerns. "The
times when I go around here screaming that I
refuse to be a slave any longer, yeah. But,"
hesitantly, "that's kind of my own doing."
Another says, "At times [I feel oppressed]. I
guess every housewife does at times, but I would
say it's not a very big thing."

As discussed earlier, getting along with
others, contributing to family and community
harmony, and not complaining or exploding are
personal qualities highly valued by the respondents . . . and by American women in general.
One observer has noted how the "unconscious desire to appear innocuous and uncontentious
predominates" among American women.[7]   Another
claims that "because of [their] subjection, wom-
en have a more fatalistic . . . view of the
world" and "the female culture has elaborated a
whole servile ethic of 'self-sacrifice.'"[8] That
self-sacrifice and a desire to be uncontentious
may be operating here is suggested by the respondents' extreme reluctance to voice complaints about their lot and the apologies which
accompany the complaints that are expressed.

The expectation that active women would be
more conscious of their oppression holds up only
slightly.   There is virtually no sense that
their ethnic background makes them victims of
injustice.   A sense of being personally kept
down is somewhat stronger among the active wom-
en, but their expression of this oppression does
not relate it particularly to the fact of their
sex. Feelings of oppression along class lines
are felt by a majority of women in each group
although they are especially strong among the
most active women. While the most active women
are somewhat more conscious of, or at least
articulate about, oppression along sex and
social class lines, the fact that the distance
between them and the other groups of women on
these measures is not great suggests that such

feelings are not the impetus behind their joining assertive community organizations.

Husbands and Social Networks.

Many of the respondents' husbands hold attitudes about appropriate sex roles which preclude an acceptance of their wives' working. Such a prohibition does not extend to their wives' moving outside the home to participate in assertive community organizations. All the women who are community activists come from homes where their husbands are at least tolerant of their participation. Most husbands are more enthusiastic than that: over 75 percent of the husbands of active women participate themselves in the activities of their wives' groups. The community organizations, by and large, attempt to solicit the membership of married couples, both husband and wife.[9] Sometimes the husband is as active as his wife. More often, he is a nominal member whose limited participation is excused by his wife on the basis that the demands of his job prohibit his taking a more active role. In contrast, none of the husbands of the inactive women belong to any community organization.

Active women, then, come from homes where the immediate family milieu is uniquely oriented toward community involvement. This suggests an important source of support for the women who are assuming this new role. Many husbands who object to their wives' working at paying jobs outside the home will not only accept but even encourage their wives' participation on a volunteer basis in assertive community organizations. The women themselves make an effort to point out that they do not receive any pay for the work they do in their organizations. Some women emphasize this each time they discuss their organizational activities. Husbands' memberships in the organizations and their acceptance of their wives' activity are indicative of fairly substantial support for the women's participation.

Having husbands who participate in organizational activities sets the active women apart from their inactive neighbors and suggests that it may be useful to examine other character- istics of husbands. Looking first at education, the husbands of the active women turn out to be considerably better educated than the husbands of the inactive women. Only 10 percent of the activists' husbands have less than a high school diploma, while 40 percent of the inactive wom- en's husbands are in this less educated category (see Table 9).

Table 9

Education of Respondents and Husbands,
by Activity Group

Group	Less Than High School		High School Graduate		Some College		College Graduate		Don't Know		Total	
	Per-cent	N	Per-cent	N	Per-cent	N	Per-cent	N	Per-cent	N	Per-cent	N
Active women	--		65	15	30	7	4	1	--		99	23
Husbands of active women	10	2	35	7	45	9	10	2	--		100	20
Inactive women	24	4	41	7	35	6	--		—		100	17
Husbands of in-active women	40	6	27	4	27	4	--		7	1	101	15

This is particularly worth noting because the education of the respondents themselves does not show such an extreme variation. Although

all the active women are at least high school
graduates and one-fourth of the inactive women
are not, if education is dichotomized, 65 percent of the women in both groups have a high
school education or less and 35 percent have at
least some college.   In other words, if the
dividing line is high school or less versus some
college or more, the two groups of women divide
up in about the same way.   With husbands, this
is not the case.   Over half of the active
women's husbands have at least some college
while only 27 percent of the inactive women's
husbands do.

The educational level of husbands may be a
more important factor in determining whether a
married woman becomes active in community organizations than the education of the woman herself.   This may reflect less tolerance of nontraditional sex role behavior on the part of
less educated men.   Or it may be that women who
become active in community organizations are
women who are generally more upwardly mobile--
much of the literature suggests that community
activists in working-class neighborhoods are
individuals already marginal to their social
class group[10] --and such women may tend to marry
better educated men.

Even more suggestive questions about the
ways in which the family environment may support
or hinder organizational participation are
raised when we look at where the respondents'
parents and their husbands' parents live.
First, respondents were asked where their own
parents live.   Again, there is little difference
between the active and the inactive women: 38
percent of the active and 33 percent of the inactive women have parents living very close by,
either in the same house or in the immediate
neighborhood (see Table 10).[11]

When respondents are asked where their
husbands' parents live, however, a strikingly
different picture emerges.   Among the active
women, only 18 percent have in-laws living in
the same neighborhood and none live in the same
house; over half live outside the Southwest Side

community altogether. Among the inactive women,
the residential pattern is totally different:
one-fifth live in the same house with their husbands' parents and an additional 50 percent have
in-laws living in the immediate neighborhood.
Only one of the inactive women is married to a
man whose parents live outside the Southwest
Side community.

Table 10

Residence of Respondents' Parents
and Husbands' Parents,
by Activity Group

Group	Parents Live in Same House		Parents Live in Same Neighbor-Hood		Parents Live on South-west Side		Parents Live outside Com-munity		Total	
	Per-cent	N	Per-cent	N	Per-cent	N	Per-cent	N	Per-cent	N
Active women	19	3	19	3	44	7	19	3	101	16
Husbands of active women	--		18	2	27	3	54	6	99	11
Inactive women	8	1	25	3	42	5	25		100	12
Husbands of in-active women	21	3	50	7	21	3	7	1	99	14

    This seems to suggest that an environment
from which her husband's family is absent is
more conducive to political activity on the part
of a working-class woman than an environment in
which her husband's family is close at hand.
Why this should be so is an intriguing question,
and one which may benefit from the theory of

social networks developed by Elizabeth Bott.[12]

Investigating the family structures of twenty urban families in London, Bott observed variations in the "connectedness" of married couples' social networks. By "connectedness" Bott means "the extent to which the people known by a family know and meet one another independently of the family."[13] Bott uses the term "close-knit" to describe "a network in which there are many relationships among the component units,"[14] that is, a social network where kin, friends, and neighbors either are the same people or interact frequently with one another. A "loose-knit" network, on the other hand, is one in which participants--friends, neighbors, and relatives--are not the same people and do not know one another. There is a tendency, observed by both Bott and other researchers, for working-class families to have relatively close-knit networks. This accounts for the strong "feelings of social similarity . . . in long established working-class areas."[15]

Bott finds that when a close-knit social network is operative for a family, there is a corresponding tendency for the husband and wife to develop a highly segregated conjugal role relationship: "Husband and wife have a clear differentiation of tasks and a considerable number of separate interests and activities."[16] In Bott's terms, there is little joint activity. This is explained as follows:

> When many of the people a person knows interact with one another, that is, when the person's network is close-knit, the members of his network tend to reach consensus on norms and they exert consistent informal pressure on one another to conform to the norms and to keep in touch with one another and, if need be, to help one another.[17]

If both a man and a woman come to a marriage with such close-knit networks:

> . . . and if conditions are such that the previous pattern of relationships is continued, the marriage will be superimposed on these pre-existing relation-

ships, and both spouses will continue to be drawn
into activities with people outside their own elementary family (family of procreation). . . . Rigid
segregation of conjugal roles will be possible
because each spouse can get help from people outside.[18]

Close-knit networks, Bott claims, are more
likely to prevail where the marital partners
have grown up or lived in the same neighborhood
for a long time. This provides the opportunity
for close and cross-cutting relationships to
develop before marriage and to be maintained
after marriage. As we have seen, the inactive
women on the average have lived in their neighborhoods longer than the active women. Furthermore, it seems safe to assume that the proximity
of parents or husbands' parents will increase
the likelihood of frequent interaction with
them, thus sustaining a close-knit social network. One woman speaks of her neighborhood
using Bott's terminology:

Oh, the neighborhood's close-knit because of my
family and my husband's family and being raised here
and he being raised here. I think it's great to live
here. . . . I haven't lived anyplace else. I'm
pleased with it. . . . I would feel fine [about
leaving] if I didn't have any of my family, but I
don't think I could go and leave my family.

On the other hand, when the social network
outside the nuclear family is "loose-knit," it
is much more likely that "a joint conjugal role
relationship" will develop between the marriage
partners. This characterizes a marriage in
which "husband and wife expect to carry out
many activities together with a minimum of
task differentiation and separation of interests."[19] Husband and wife will look to each
other for support, and segregation of activities
along sex lines will be less rigid.

It appears that the active women may live
within a somewhat more loose-knit social network; at least one segment of their kin--their
husbands' parents--are not their neighbors. A
joint conjugal role relationship also seems more

characteristic of the active women. All but one
of them speak of their husbands' sharing in the
activities of the community organizations with
them. If it is true that their social network
is more loose-knit, this may help explain why
these women are the ones who have become involved in the assertive community organizations. A close-knit network, supporting a traditional pattern of sex role segregation, would
not allow women to participate in organizational
activity of a political nature since this has
not been viewed as a component of a woman's
role.

There is, however, one major deviation from
what this network theory would predict: it is
only the proximity of the husband's parents that
seems to make a difference. Why should it be
that a woman's assuming a nontraditional role is
more difficult in an environment where her husband's family is present? Men in general and
working-class men in particular have been found
to be more conservative with respect to women's
roles than are women themselves.[20] A husband,
discouraging of nontraditional behavior for his
wife and supported in his judgment by nearby
parents and other members of a close-knit social
network, may present an obstacle to his wife's
assuming a new role that is nearly insurmount-
able. It may also be that the husband himself
is subjected to constraints on his behavior when
his parents are nearby. The process may be an
indirect one: the husband, pressured to preserve the norms of the close-knit network, is
unable to pass on to his wife support sufficient
to allow her to move into a nontraditional role.
Whatever the dynamic, the presence in the neighborhood of her husband's parents seems to have a
real, albeit unrecognized, impact on whether or
not a woman becomes politically active.

Any application of social network theory to
these respondents is, of course, based on certain assumptions. There is no detailed
knowledge of the actual social networks of these
couples; nor does the geographical proximity of
either parents or in-laws necessarily mean that

they are a part of that network. There is, however,a striking difference between the active
and the inactive women on the variable of in-law
residence, and social network theory, to the
extent that it helps us make sense of the
effects of this difference, is useful.

Furthermore, to the extent that our assumptions about the differences in the social
networks of the two groups of respondents are
accurate, this finding has clear implications
for future changes in the social roles of
working-class women. As more working-class
neighborhoods in urban areas are uprooted--
because of racial change, urban renewal, or the
costs of living in the city--families moving
into new neighborhoods will necessarily find
their old close-knit networks attenuated. With
the development of more loose-knit social networks, role segregation may become less rigid,
even if the social class position of the family
does not change. This is a process distinct
from changes in behavior that occur as families
move from the working class to the middle class.
Such social mobility is neither likely for nor
desired by many working-class families like
those in this sample. Rather, this suggests
that changes in behavior will unwittingly result
from the lifting of constraints imposed by a
certain social network. Women (and men, as
well, one suspects) will, in a more loose-knit
social network, one without a deep normative
tradition, be more free to take on new roles
than they have been in the past, and activities
shared by husband and wife will become more common. More generally, this implies that a
weakening of old networks may be a necessary
pre-condition for the establishment of new networks, built on new relationships and new norms.

No single factor, determinative of why some
women become active in assertive community organizations and others do not, emerges from the
analysis in this chapter and the preceding
chapter. Rather, what does emerge are the
dimensions of a process whereby a number of
factors, at different times, influence a woman

in a particular situation and move her to become involved. Extrapolating from the specific findings, we can create an ideal-typical model which shows how this process operates. This model, Figure 2, is an ideal type because "the construcure in itself is like a utopia . . . arrived at by the analytical accentuation of certain elements of reality."[21] Although this model is not in itself a description of the process any one woman went through, it is valuable for, in Weber's words, "heuristic as well as expository purposes."[22]

The time sequence portrayed in Figure 2 is conceptual rather than empirical. The particular time sequence, along with the specified elements, may vary for any given activist.

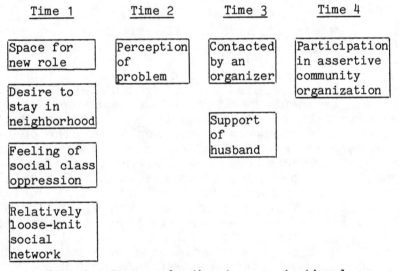

Fig. 2. Process leading to organizational
participation

The woman who is a potential candidate for community activist has several important factors already operative in her life situation as represented at Time 1: 1) she has space in her life for a new role; 2) she has a strong emotional attachment to and desire to stay in her neighborhood; 3) she has feelings that people in her social class are treated unfairly;

and 4) she lives within a relatively loose-knit social network.

The woman has space in her life for a new role because she has neither small children at home nor a paying job. She has time to assume the activities and responsibilities that the role of community activist might entail. She also has a strong attachment to the neighbor-hood, evidenced by the fact that she does not want to move out and that she would feel very sad if she did have to leave. In addition, she expresses the belief that people in her social class are treated unfairly. And, finally, she lives within a social environment from which her husband's parents are absent, suggesting that her network of friends, family, and neighbors may be less close-knit than that of the inactive women.

A woman in such a life situation is con-fronted by a problem (Time 2). She becomes increasingly annoyed by the pollutants ema-nating from a nearby factory, or she gradually realizes that racial change in her neighborhood is an imminent reality, or a newspaper story reveals that an expressway is scheduled for con-struction a block away from her home. The prob-lem becomes a matter of conscious concern. As concern emerges, she may begin to develop a position or perspective on the issue. But still she is not moved to confront the problem actively. Most working-class women, and about two-thirds of the respondents here, have had no education beyond high school. As well, they have limited job experiences and those with children have often been out of the job market for a number of years. Consequently, they are somewhat timorous about taking upon themselves any role which would entail meeting new people in an untested capacity, and especially one which might demand a public demonstration of a particular competence or set of skills.

In this ideal typical model, two additional factors, represented at Time 3, will provide the necessary impetus to move a woman from a state of readiness and concern to a state of active participation. These factors are: the support of her husband, and being contacted by a leader or organizer of the community group. The encouragement that both of these individuals can offer seems especially crucial at this particular point in helping a woman decide to assume her new role.

A husband's support, measured in this analysis by his being active in the group as well as by his wife's assessment of how he feels, is probably essential for most of these women. The women of this community tend to hold fairly traditional views about what behavior is appropriate for them. If encouragement from husbands is lacking, most women are likely to feel uncertain and perhaps guilty about moving into a nontraditional role. Encouragement from the husband appears more likely to be forthcoming if his parents do not live in the immediate neighborhood.

Even if there should be family support for the idea of such participation, it will not become a reality until someone from the group reaches out to encourage the woman to participate. If a woman's husband is active in the organization, he can play this role as well, although this seldom seems to be the case. Such a contact can assure a woman not only that her participation is valued, but also that she will know at least one other person in the group and, therefore, not feel totally isolated should she decide to join. It is at this point that community organizers, moving into working-class neighborhoods in increased numbers over the last decade, have met and responded to stirrings in the women residing in these neighborhoods. Well-trained community organizers fully recognize that reluctant citizens often have to be coaxed into joining an organization.

Finally, the culmination of the effects of all the preceding steps is realized at Time 4: the woman begins to participate in an assertive community organization. Although a woman may become an active member of such an organization when one or more of the variables in the model are absent from her particular situation--and some of these women have--it would appear, on the basis of the data explored here, that the absence of any one variable will reduce the probability of her becoming active. Similarly, the addition of each variable will increase the likelihood of her becoming involved. It remains for future research to determine the relative importance of each variable in the model.

[VI]

Community Activism
and the Feminist Movement

In the first chapter, some of the shifts in political and social attitudes of recent years which have made this particular period ripe for political activism in urban working-class communities were noted. In Chapters IV and V, the political, psychological, and structural forces particular to certain women's lives which preceded their entrance into assertive community organizations were discussed. But, thus far, little explicit attention has been paid to the women's liberation movement, a major aspect of the broader cultural context within which this new role has emerged.

There is a perspective from which it may be legitimate to view the adoption of a new political role by working-class women as one more expression of the broader feminist movement. The 1970s are a time when women's roles in general are being questioned, re-evaluated, and restructured as they have not been since the earlier feminist movement at the turn of the century. Nonetheless, such a view by itself would not be true to the women's own evaluation of their activities and the changes they have experienced.

To the extent that the women's liberation movement is something that has happened <u>to</u> women, it is certainly happening to working-class women as well as to others. Changes in media portrayals of women, the access of women to jobs previously reserved for men, more wide-spread acceptance of divorce, contraception, and abortion, and the more equitable distri-bution of rights, wages, and opportunities which lawsuits have begun to bring about--these have happened to all women and have become a part of everyone's lives. But to the extent that the women's liberation movement is a subjective ex-perience, including a consciousness sensitized to oppression, a changed view of oneself and the distribution of power in the society, and a willingness to struggle to change traditional aspects of women's lives--to this extent, the women's movement is not something most of these women have experienced.

One fact that readily emerges from the data is the respondents' dissociation from what they see as the organized feminist movement. "Well, I'm not a believer in the women's lib movement," says one very active woman in response to a question about why she pursues her activities so vigorously. "I think it's absolutely stupid be-cause women don't know how well off they are." After a brief pause, she adds, "However, if this country is to be saved at all, it'll be the wom-en who do it."

This woman's remarks point out a curious juxtaposition of attitudes which underlies the respondents' feelings about women and their par-ticipation in political activities. On the whole, they view the feminist movement as of only limited value. It is perceived as relevant in some ways to unmarried women who have to sup-port themselves and perhaps valuable for what it is doing in terms of guaranteeing women equal pay for equal work. But, certainly, the women who are active in their communities do not in any way see their activity as part of a quest for their personal liberation.

At the same time, they share a sense of their importance, an overwhelming conviction that if the problems of the community are to be solved, it will be they, the women, who solve

them. This is largely because women have more
time than men:

> Women have more time to go to meetings. The man is
> the breadwinner. He has to report to work and he
> can't be reporting everywhere else, and has to ful-
> fill his job. I think it's the women on these issues
> who have to take the stand. We need men, but they can
> only give so much of their time.

It is also because women are closer to the
community and its concerns than men, as another
active women explains: "We have the contact in
the community. . . . my husband doesn't know the
number of people in the community that I know
just by virtue of involvement in the school."

Women appear willing to assume the burden
of resolving community problems by default. Men
are too busy with their jobs and, moreover,
playing this kind of political role might pose
some risks to a man's job. One woman whose husband is employed by the city as a policeman explained that she first became active when her
husband wanted to campaign for a non-Democratic
candidate but could not do so without risk of
being fired. She campaigned for the candidate on
behalf of her husband and thus began her own
involvement in community activities. Others
allude to similar concerns: "For my husband, to
be involved in the community, it's jeopardizing
a little bit of that security he has. . . . I
don't think they can take the chance that a
woman can take."

These reasons of time, community contacts,
and lesser vulnerability combine in the eyes of
the respondents to create a situation in which
women can, and indeed must, resolve community
problems. Almost 90 percent of both the active
and inactive groups claim that women can resolve
the problems in the community (see Table 11).

While the active women's affirmation of the
efficacy of their sex does not differentiate
them from the inactive women, they do respond to
the question with different emphases. Some of
the active women will buttress their response by

referring to the reactions of corporate and public officials which they have witnessed in their
confrontations.

Table 11

Responses to: "Can Women Resolve These
        Problems?"   by Activity Group

Group	Yes		No Men Should		Men and Women Should Work Together		Total	
	Per-cent	N	Per-cent	N	Per-cent	N	Per-cent	N
Active women	86	19	9	2	4	1	99	22
Inactive women	87	13	--		13	2	100	15

I think they're afraid of us. When a bunch of women
go down there and start hollering, they really take
notice. They don't like it. I don't think they like
to hear women out there screaming and hollering or
even just walking around with signs.

The women who are very active almost invariably add a disclaimer to their positive
response to the question, a disclaimer which
either dissociates them from the feminist movement or, more frequently, states their belief
that men should be resolving the problems and
they would be happier if the men were doing so.
One active woman, for example, says: "Women
have to get involved. I believe they have to.
But," she quickly adds, "I'm not for women's
liberation."   Another woman who has been very
active in her group since its inception says:

Ideally, it would be better for a man to do it. . . .
It seems men have, not all men, a lot of men, just
don't want to be bothered and I feel it really should
be a man's responsibility. . . .   I think they're
stronger than women. At least they should be. I
think they're much more clear thinking, more logical,
than a woman. . . .

These qualifying statements, coming as they do almost solely from the active women, suggest a tension which several times becomes evident for the most active respondents. They are the ones most intensely involved in nontra- ditional behaviors--activities such as demon- strations, public speaking, and confrontations with elected officials; at the same time, they verbally adhere more strongly than the other women to a conservative view of sex roles. It is of note that the only two respondents who unequivocally claim that men, not women, should resolve the problems are women who are them- selves intensely involved in such activities. It may be that such verbal adherences to tradi- tional norms provide this group of women with reassurance that their new activities are not moving them too much beyond the realm of accept- able behavior or at least, if there is such movement, that it is based on temporary exigen- cies rather than any deep-seated rejection of traditional values.

While there exists this strong conviction that women can resolve problems at a community level, there is some uncertainty about whether the country would be better off if more women held political office. Still, a majority of women believe that the entrance of more women into politics would bring about change: 75 per- cent of the inactive women and 65 percent of the active women believe this (see Table 12). And, invariably, the expectation is that the changes would be positive and the country would be better off with more women holding political power.

The reasons upon which this belief is based are strikingly reminiscent of arguments presented at the beginning of the century to buttress the case for women's suffrage. Notions that women are more compassionate than men, more concerned about people and their welfare, less militaristic, and less driven by selfish pursuits are proffered now as they were then.[1] "Well," says one inactive respondent, "I would hope that there wouldn't be as many wars.

Women have a lot more compassion and understanding." Similarly, a very active woman
thinks "the interests of women would not be so
militaristic as men and they would see the need
for helping people that needed help. . . . Women
have more feel for people and their needs." The
belief that women are more compassionate than
men persists today, despite the disillusion-
ments experienced forty years ago when American
society did not change in a markedly more humane
direction as a result of women's enfranchise-
ment. The persistence of such beliefs about
what could be if women had equal decision-making
power attests to the fact that the actual political role of women has not changed much since
1920.

Table 12

Responses to: "Would the Country Be Different
If There Were More Women In Political
Office?" by Activity Group

Group	Yes		No		Ambivalent or Don't know		Total	
	Per-cent	N	Per-cent	N	Per-cent	N	Per-cent	N
Active women	65	15	13	3	22	5	100	23
Inactive women	75	12	12	2	12	2	99	16

The belief that women possess a unique
potential for purifying politics is embedded in
a more basic notion that men and women are inherently different and so will have different
ways of viewing and dealing with problems.
"Women have a different perspective, would see
things differently than men." "I believe that
women have a motherly instinct." "I think women
are more honest than men." "Women, as a rule,
are not as stubborn and as harsh and as de-
manding as a man is." Upon such beliefs is
predicated the conviction that more women in

political office would result in more humane
social practices throughout the country.   A
belief that there are differences of emotion,
instinct, and perspective between men and women
here provides an argument for supporting women
in political office.   Because of the unique
traits characteristic of each sex, if there were
more women involved there would be two different
viewpoints and responses, "so the whole would be
better."

A few of the women do not voice such an
argument; they are the ones who are not convinced that the entrance of women into politics
would make much difference. These women believe
that involvement in the political process will
have the same kind of influence on females as it
does on males.   "I really kind of think that
you're going to fall into the same political
trap that the man falls into. You know, favors
for favors. . . . I don't think it would be any
more effective or any less effective."   For
these few women, there is no mystique.   The
active women are slightly more likely than the
inactive to be ambivalent or uncertain about
whether or not the country really would be any
different. Their greater uncertainty may derive
from the fact that they have seen women playing
roles which in the broadest sense are political
in their community organizations and, perhaps,
have not seen them acting in ways very different
from men. One active women puts it this way:

> I really don't know. I don't know if the women would
> tend to do the same things the men are doing or if
> they'd be strong enough to resist outside influence.
> I have the feeling that women would tend to do about
> the same thing as the men, I really do. You know,
> it's only natural to get your point you give a little
> something, so I don't think there'd be that much
> difference.

The notion of more women holding political
office (especially in certain areas--"when
you're dealing with legislation that has to do
with very young children," for example) has a
certain attraction to the respondents. And a
majority are even inclined to believe that a

woman could hold the country's highest office.
About three-fourths of the women in both groups
believe a woman could someday become President.

The response of one woman is typical of
those who see the possibility of a woman's
becoming President. "I think that some day
there could be [a woman President]. There's
been so many other changes that I wouldn't cross
it out." Several note that a Catholic made it
and so probably could a woman. Most of those
who do not think a woman could make it attribute
this to the difficulties men would pose. "No, I
don't think she'd ever get elected," says one
active woman, "because the men would never support her and they're the ones who control all
the machinery and all the workings that she'd
need."

While there is little difference between
the groups in terms of those who see the possibility of a female President, when it comes to
actually voting for a woman, there is a substantial difference. Over four-fifths of the active
women claim they would vote for a woman candidate who was running for President, but barely
half of the inactive women would do so (see
Table 13). Some who admit the possibility of a
woman's becoming President would not themselves
vote for one. "No, I don't think I would vote
for a woman," says one inactive respondent.
"She'd be too soft. I mean, a woman's too emotional . . . I don't think that would be good."

Table 13

Responses to: "Would You Vote For A Woman
For President?" by Activity Group

Group	Yes		No/Don't Know		Total	
	Per-cent	N	Per-cent	N	Per-cent	N
Active women	81	13	19	3	100	16
Inactive women	54	7	46	6	100	13

Respondents discussed how they would feel if somehow a woman should become President. Most expressed a fairly neutral reaction to such a possibility: it would be okay or it would depend on the individual and her particular qualifications. "I don't think it would make that much difference to me" is a typical response. A number of women, however, reacted more strongly. A few were very enthusiastic about the idea; more were strongly against such an occurrence.

Who are the women for whom the idea of a female in such a position of power represents something especially negative or especially positive? As Table 14 indicates, 25 percent of the sample express strong hostility toward the idea of a woman becoming President. Almost one-third of the very active women are in this most negative group; fewer of the inactive and only one somewhat active woman express such hostility. The basis of the negative feelings is invariably the belief that certain behaviors are appropriate to men and certain behaviors are appropriate to women and the Presidency of the United States is unquestionably a man's job. Most of the respondents who see the situation negatively indicate that they would be terribly dismayed at such a breakdown in the established order.

> I don't want to see us get that strong . . . God did not put us on earth for that. The man always carries the spear, not the woman. If we become so strong and masculine, we cease to be women.

Calling upon God and the natural order of things is typical:

> I can't see a woman there, just like I can't see a woman being Pope. . . . To me, there are certain places for men . . . God was a man, his apostles were men, and he more or less gave it to men, this honor or job to do. . . . He was trying to show that men should have more, well not superiority, but there should be a certain level where men are a little higher and have certain jobs and women should have certain jobs.

Table 14

Responses to: "How Would You Feel If A Woman
Did Somehow Become President?"
by Activity Group

Group	Positive Response		Neutral Response		Negative Response		Total	
	Per-cent	N	Per-cent	N	Per-cent	N	Per-cent	N
Very active women	12	2	56	9	31	5	99	16
Somewhat active women	--		83	5	17	1	100	16
Inactive women	7	1	71	10	21	3	99	14

Typical also is the noting of certain of women's "weaknesses."   "I don't think women should be in politics . . . I don't think women have the stamina that men do.   I just don't think it's a job for women."

The few women who are particularly enthusiastic are so for different reasons.   The one strong supporter of a female President who is not an active member of an assertive community organization is herself an unusually impressive woman.   She thinks "it would be great" if a woman became President, and expresses an eagerness to see women active in all areas of society.   With only a high school education and raising 12 children on her truck driver husband's salary, she has already sent three of her daughters to college.

One of the active women, the only one who had been involved in anti-war activities, supports the idea because "it could help a lot; we wouldn't have war."   The other active woman has a very different reason for believing "it might be a good thing."   She believes "if a

woman could get in there, as a typical housewife, when they have their news conferences,
they'd be exchanging recipes and sewing patterns, and if there's any problems they would be
ironed out."

These two active women, despite the extreme
difference in their expressions of concern, have
similarly idealistic notions about the potential effects of women in power. These notions
are similar to those that were mentioned earlier
when respondents were asked about the effects on
the country of more women in office. There is
little in fact to suggest that the world's problems could be "ironed out" with an exchange of
recipes, or that there would be no more wars if
women held high office. Such ideas indicate
little understanding of the real concentrations
and consequences of power in the United States.
As well, they show the persistence of certain
stereotypes about women. The notion that
women's attention could eliminate international
conflict is myth, incorporating a "super-woman"
fantasy. "To assume . . . that woman could
succeed in purifying something which is not
susceptible of purification, is to credit her
with supernatural powers," observed Emma
Goldman years ago.[2]

This is not to say that there are no ob-
servable differences between male and female
political behaviors. Male politicians have been
characterized as engaging in a form of "machismo" confrontation which is not found among
female politicians.[3] Females have been found
to be more opposed than men to institutional
violence.[4] And women were considerably less
likely than men to be "hawkish" on the Vietnam
War.[5] There are differences, but they are
likely the result of the impact of cultural expectations.

Most of the respondents argue for neither a
biologically nor sociologically determined difference between the sexes in the area of politics. Most hold to the position that things
would be about the same with a woman president
as they are with a man. Or they argue that

variations would depend on the individual qualities of the woman, not her sex. This perspective is well phrased by one woman who is
somewhat active in her group:

> I don't think it would be too much different.
> . . . She's gotta be just as intelligent as any other
> President and she's gotta have the same advisers.
> She's not gonna be standing there all by herself.

A tendency noted earlier persists in these
responses: women who are most active are also
most likely to adhere to a position which reflects conflict in their ideas about appropriate
behavior for females. In this case, those women
who have the most political influence themselves
and are in a position where they could at least
potentially gain some power are the ones who
express the most hostile reactions to the idea
of a woman in a position of power.

In summary, the prevailing opinion is that
the country would be better off if more women
held national office but that women are particularly suited for certain offices, such as those
that concern themselves with children and
schools. There is some reluctance, markedly
evident among the inactive women, to support a
woman for President. There is also a notable
ambivalence among the active women about the extent to which it is "right" for a woman to hold
the highest political office.

What underlies these ideas about women in
politics? What are the more fundamental notions
about women and men and the relationships between them that provide the basis for the political views expressed here?

To tap sex-role attitudes each woman was
asked to respond to a battery of items borrowed
from a questionnaire developed by Sandra Ball-
Rokeach.[6] The seven statements, listed in
Table 15 along with the responses, were read to
the women who were then asked to indicate the
extent of their agreement with each.

Item 1, which claims that "women are as
capable of being good leaders in industry,

politics, education, or science as men," finds all but one of the active women in agreement and two-thirds of them in strong agreement. Among inactive women, on the other hand, one-fifth disagree; only 40 percent are in strong agreement. The majority of inactive women are not convinced that women are as capable as men of being good leaders; this may explain why the inactive group is less willing to cast their vote for a woman for President.

This item, which calls for support for the idea that women are able to play a strong leadership role in the political realm (along with other extrafamilial realms) is more vigorously supported by those women who have themselves been active in politically oriented activities. This is not very surprising. What is surprising, however, is the way in which active women's support of nontraditional female behavior drastically falls off in other areas.

The very active women are least likely of all three activity groups to agree that wives should have as much say as their husbands in making important family decisions, least likely to feel strongly that a woman who decides not to get married can be a perfectly normal person and adequate woman, least likely to believe that women who do the same work as men should get the same salary, least likely to believe it would be a good thing if more married couples decided not to have children, and least likely to agree that a decision about having an abortion should be left solely to the woman involved. It is only on the question of whether schools should pay more attention to preparing boys for careers than girls that the most active women once again emerge as having a stronger pro-female perspective than the inactive women, and even then the difference is slight.

Excluding for the moment the item on equal pay for equal work, all the areas in which the most active women emerge as most traditional or least supportive of women expanding their options are areas which relate to women's roles in the family--specifically, marriage, family decision-making, and having children.

Table 15

Responses to Items on Women's Roles

Group	Agree Strongly		Agree Somewhat		Disagree Somewhat		Disagree Strongly		Total	
	Per-cent	N	Per-cent	N	Per-cent	N	Per-cent	N	Per-cent	N
1. "Women are as capable of being good leaders in industry, politics, education or science as men."										
Very active	69	11	25	4	6	1	--	--	100	16
Somewhat active	67	4	33	2	--	--	--	--	100	6
Inactive	40	6	40	6	13	2	7	1	100	15
2. "A wife should have as much say as her husband in making the important decisions affecting their family."										
Very active	60	9	33	5	7	1	--	--	100	15
Somewhat active	83	5	17	1	--	--	--	--	100	6
Inactive	100	16	--	--	--	--	--	--	100	16
3. "A woman who decides not to get married can be a perfectly normal person and adequate woman."										
Very active	53	8	47	1	--	--	--	--	100	15
Somewhat active	100	6	--	--	--	--	--	--	100	6
Inactive	94	15	6	1	--	--	--	--	100	16

Table 15--Continued

Group	Agree Strongly Per-cent	Agree Strongly N	Agree Somewhat Per-cent	Agree Somewhat N	Disagree Somewhat Per-cent	Disagree Somewhat N	Disagree Strongly Per-cent	Disagree Strongly N	Total Per-cent	Total N
4. "Women should get paid the same salary as men who do the same work, even if the woman is single and the man has a family."										
Very active	69	11	25	4	6	1	--	--	100	16
Somewhat active	100	6	--	--	--	--	--	--	100	6
Inactive	75	12	12	2	12	2	--	--	99	16
5. "It would be a good thing if more married couples decided not to have children."										
Very active	6	1	25	4	12	2	56	9	99	16
Somewhat active	17	1	33	2	33	2	17	1	100	6
Inactive	6	1	31	5	12	2	50	8	99	16
6. "Whether or not to have an abortion is a decision which should be left entirely to the woman involved."										
Very active	23	3	8	1	31	4	38	5	100	13
Somewhat active	17	1	50	3	--	--	33	2	100	6
Inactive	33	5	27	4	13	2	27	4	100	15
7. "Schools should pay more attention to preparing boys for careers than girls."										
Very active	--	--	28	4	21	3	50	7	99	14
Somewhat active	--	--	17	1	--	--	83	5	100	6
Inactive	12	2	19	3	19	3	50	8	99	16

Item 2, "A wife should have as much say as her husband in making the important decisions affecting their family," shows this pattern. Very active women are the least likely to agree strongly, while the inactive women show unanimous support for the idea. The three activity groups do not differ in the extent to which they support women's having equal power in the political realm, but the inactive respondents are considerably more supportive of the wife's having equal power in the domestic realm. This difference may be due to the fact that a greater proportion of the inactive women are working at paying jobs outside the home. Working wives tend to have more actual power in the family, vis-a-vis their husbands, than non-working wives. A gain in domestic power follows a gain in economic power.

The same shift toward the wife's having more power in the home has been found by researchers to take place where the wife participates in organizational activities, provided she is more active than her husband. The increase in her power cancels out only if her husband's participation is equal to or greater than her own. This may happen when interpersonal behavior is measured. Unfortunately, no such measures of actual behavior are available for this sample. But the attitudes of the Southwest Side women do not lend support to such an argument. All of the active women who are in less than strong agreement with the idea of wives having equal power are more active in community organizations than their husbands. It is impossible to gauge whether or not they actually have domestic power equal to their husbands. But their claim is that women should not.

The other question which these results pose is why the inactive women should be so supportive of domestic egalitarianism. If the inactive women are more representative of the traditional working class, it may well be that the family domain is more readily defined as the woman's sphere for them. Indeed, for traditional working-class families the issue might not be whether the wife should have an equal say in family decisions but whether the husband should have an equal say.

Rainwater and Handel claim that, as the traditional working-class family moves toward more emphasis on the nuclear family, the husband will begin to "define himself as a more involved person [in the family]" and will "expect to participate more actively in family decision making and . . . leave fewer things up to his wife."[9] There is evidence that the active women and their husbands are more likely to have joint conjugal roles; certainly we see evidence of this in the fact that husbands and wives tend to belong to the same assertive community organizations. Given this reality and the fact that there are more shared activities among the couples where the women are active, why are these women less supportive of egalitarian domestic decision-making?

Women who have moved into active community roles may feel ambivalent about expending a large amount of time and energy outside the family and therefore may attempt to resolve their discomfort by verbally adhering to a position in which they concede their subservience to their husbands. This interpretation is supported by the need displayed by the active women constantly to reaffirm to others that their major commitment is to their home and family and that, despite their outside activities, they are not neglecting their domestic responsibilities.

The very active women are least willing to accept the assertion that "a woman who decides not to get married can be a perfectly normal person and adequate women" (Table 15, Item 3). Almost half of the very active women only agree "somewhat" with this, indicating that they have some doubts about the normality of the single state for women. There is virtually unanimous strong agreement from the less active and the inactive respondents. Again the very active women appear to be adhering in an overly rigid fashion to traditional sex roles, in this case to the idea that female fulfillment is found only in marriage.

Items 5 and 6 both suggest alternatives to having children, the former suggesting that married couples refrain from having children, the latter supporting a woman's right to make her own decision about whether or not to have an abortion. On both of these items the very active women are the least willing to allow women these alternatives. Two-thirds of the very active women do not agree with the idea that it would "be a good thing if more married couples decided not to have children." Fifty percent of the somewhat actives and 62 percent of the inactives also disagree, so the differences among groups are not great but they are part of a consistent trend.

On the abortion item differences are greater: 69 percent of the very active do not feel an abortion should be a woman's personal decision and more than half hold "strongly" to this view. Only one-third of the somewhat active women and 40 percent of the inactive women do not support a woman's right to decide about an abortion. One woman who is very active, in the course of talking about her life, speaks of being pregnant "every two years." "I was very unhappy; I really was. But I think that's a woman, though. Then there's an adjustment . . . I think it's all part of being a woman, I really do."

Item 4, "Women should get paid the same salary as men who do the same work, even if the woman is single and the man has a family," has as its major referent a work role. Again, the very active women are somewhat less liberal in their responses than the other groups: 69 percent of the very actives strongly support the position of equal pay for equal work, while 75 percent of the inactives and 100 percent of the somewhat actives do so. Even in this area, the one which many women named as an area where they and the women's liberation movement might have something in common, there is a residue of uncertainty among both the very active and the inactive respondents.

Disagreement with the last item given to respondents, "Schools should pay more attention to preparing boys for careers than girls," would support the notion that females are as suited and as entitled to prepare for and enter careers as are males. A majority in each group does take this position. The inactive women are most likely to believe that boys should have preferential treatment in schooling (31 percent); there is slightly less support for this idea among the very active women (28 percent) and the somewhat active women (17 percent).

Leaving aside for the moment that group of women who are somewhat active, a definite pattern emerges in the responses of the other two groups. Those women who are very active in assertive community organizations emerge as more supportive of the idea of women as leaders in various fields and of schools giving girls career preparation equal to boys. When it comes to family-related roles, however, the active women take a considerably less feminist position than the inactive. The inactive women are more likely than the very active to believe that a wife should have equal say in family decisions, more likely to believe that a woman can refrain from marriage and lead a normal life, slightly more likely to believe it would be a good thing if fewer married couples had children, and considerably more likely to believe that abortion should be a woman's own decision. The equal pay for equal work item shows little difference between the groups but the item itself touches on both extrafamilial and domestic areas by adding the proviso "even if the woman is single and the man has a family."

If a nontraditional sex role orientation is defined as one in which there is support for females being accorded treatment equal to males and for females having a variety of options regarding life style and life choices legitimately accessible to them, then the inactive women are

more nontraditional than the active with respect
to family roles and more traditional with respect to extrafamilial roles.

This presents an apparent paradox. Are
women with such an orientation, one which is
simultaneously supportive of traditional family
roles and nontraditional extrafamilial roles,
more attracted to assertive community organizations? Or does the participation itself produce
conflict about role preferences which, by way of
resolution, leads the active women to express a
strong adherence to traditional familial roles
even as they may actually be moving away from
them? The bulk of evidence suggests that much
of the active women's verbal support of traditional roles, given as it often is to very
conservative positions on family and sex roles,
belies their attempts and those of their husbands to come to grips with the issue of what is
acceptable behavior for a wife and mother. A
woman who holds a leadership position in one of
the assertive community orgnizations (inciden-
tally, she is not one of our sample) has been
sued for divorce by her husband, who contends
that she has ceased being a proper wife, mother,
and housekeeper since becoming intensely involved in the activities of the organization.
The woman claims this is not so and continues to
assert that her primary commitment is to her
family. Nonetheless, the amount of time and
energy that she expends on organizational
activities has opened this to question, both to
her husband and, painfully, to herself.

Commitment to and involvement in extrafamilial activities need not raise any doubt
about family commitments, and in many families
where a wife's career or other activities outside the home are taken for granted the doubts
are absent or at least less intense. The
families in this sample, however, have not experienced a tradition in which women's loyalties
may be legitimately divided; commitment to one
realm may automatically call into question commitment to another.

It is difficult to say anything about the

somewhat active women, since they are such a small group. They emerge as the most liberal in support of women not marrying and not having children; they also are most liberal on the issue of equal pay for women and equal career preparation for girls. They do not show a pattern as distinct as that for either of the other groups.

The very active women are overwhelmingly likely to believe that women are treated unfairly in this country. This further compounds the paradoxical position on women and their roles which they seem to hold. Despite their adherence to a traditional ideology with respect to women in the family, a full 88 percent believe women generally are accorded unfair treatment (see Table 16). A close 83 percent of the somewhat active women take this position, but only 69 percent of those who are inactive do so.

Table 16

Responses to: "Are Women Treated Unfairly in This Country?" by Activity Group

Group	Yes		No/Don't Know		Total	
	Per-cent	N	Per-cent	N	Per-cent	N
Very active women	88	14	12	2	100	16
Somewhat active women	83	5	17	1	100	6
Inactive women	69	11	31	5	100	16

Evidence of "unfair" treatment derives primarily from the way women are treated in the world outside the home. There is little reference to unfair treatment within the family. Most often the basis for believing there is unfair treatment is job discrimination:

. . . as far as job employment, women don't get the

promotions that men do. I know an example right in
the family of a woman that's doing all the work in her
office and the men are out playing golf and she's
doing all the work and . . . she's never gotten a
promotion since she's been there, and she deserves
it. . . .

Although there is more sensitivity to the
ways in which women are treated unfairly among
the active women, only a couple of them specify
inequities within the political realm. One of
those who does touch on that area mentions
the "general idea that women are not responsible":

> . . . many people have that idea. Even on this block.
> I don't think the people on this block would ever
> elect a woman block president. Women and men are
> put into certain roles . . . like on this block,
> women take care of education, a man shouldn't bother
> with that. A man should bother with police, the
> buildings. . . .

One of the few active women who sees no
unfair treatment presents her reasons:

> I think women have it pretty good. I know I do. I've
> always felt that women have always, ah, been able to
> do anything they really wanted to do. Well, like this
> girl's going to this all boys' college. Now to me, my
> own feeling, I wouldn't want to go there. I really
> wouldn't.

Earlier most of the respondents emerged as
women who do not view themselves as personally
oppressed or kept down in any way. Yet, here,
when the issue is framed in general, not personal, terms, most respondents agree that women
are indeed treated unfairly on the basis of
their sex.

It has been said that women "appear to have
no consciousness of the causal connections between their life chances and the stratification
system special to their society."[10] It is true
that the women in this sample appear to have no
consciousness of, or at least no willingness to
verbalize, how their particular life chances
have been muted by the fact of their sex. But

they do have a clear recognition that women's
lot in general in this society is an unfair one.
Rather than extend this notion of unfair treatment to their own lives, the tendency is to
believe that marriage has saved them from the
inequities heaped upon the single woman, and a
good man has saved them from an unhappy fate at
the hands of an unfair husband. "I've been
liberated. I have a very good husband. He lets
out so much rope."

When the discussion of unfair treatment of
women extended to the feminist movement, there
was among this group only the limited support
noted earlier. When asked how they feel about
the women's movement, respondents' answers
ranged from "I'm not for women's lib too much"
to "It's all hogwash" to "I think there's a
great move to break down the whole concept of
what a home is all about and what a woman's role
is." Only one woman expressed strong support--
"they're doing a lot of good in just making
women aware"--although she also stressed that
she did not think she could ever bring herself
to participate in any organized activities or
demonstrations.   Several other women, both
active and inactive, showed qualified support
for some aspects of the women's movement:

I see it as a conglomeration of many combined attitudes. . . . I think there are women in the women's
liberation movement who feel strongly that everything
should be right down the line; women should go to war
if men go to war. But others think, and this would be
my view, it's a little more realistic view, that
there are certain things that women should have
equality in . . . not being discriminated against,
say, in buying a house or renting an apartment. . . .

There is strong recognition of the need to
adjust sex-based economic inequities, and to the
extent that the feminist movement does that, it
is supported. Beyond that the movement is
either dismissed as ridiculous ("these ones that
are going into these all-men lunch rooms and
things like that, I think they have little to do
. . . and as far as drafting ladies and all
that, I think they're all nuts, if they want

that") or, more frequently, rejected because it threatens to break down familiar and approved male and female roles.

> The only thing I agree with them on is as far as the job situation, but other than that a woman is a woman and a man is a man as far as I'm concerned. I like being a woman so why, uh, I wouldn't want to be a man. . . . What the heck, I like having the door opened for me and stuff like that. . . .

Sometimes the distinction between the sexes is based on emotional as well as social differences:

> I think it demeans the role of wife and mother. . . . It's not even intelligent to say you want to be equal with men because women are different . . . I think we were created for a special role in life . . . you can't equalize men and women. They are emotionally, physically different. They're different. There are certain tasks that women are not emotionally able to cope with. . . .

According to another woman, the threat is not so much to inherent differences between men and women as to the role to which women like herself are committed: "They're trying to change the 'Mrs.' thing to begin with, all these things that stand for the married woman, they're trying to wipe away. And I don't go for that and I don't think most married women do."

The women of the Southwest Side have been exposed to only a limited and often a distorted view of what feminism is all about. Nonetheless, they are able to sort out for themselves various strands of the movement and accept some aspects while rejecting others.[11]

Reflecting on the extent to which women should be politically active and can be politically effective, these respondents see things differently depending on whether they are referring to participation at a local level or participation at a level beyond the immediate community. There is a conviction, shared by all respondents, that women can be effective on a neighborhood level and must assume the burden of neighborhood problems if changes are to take place. School conditions and shifts in the neighborhood racial composition are the issues which moved the active women to participate in the first place and they have had some experiences which have fed their feelings of political efficacy on the local level. But even the inactive women recognize that women are closer to the community and its problems and so must be the ones to resolve them.

Beyond the level of the immediate community, the problems to be dealt with are less tangible, the ways of resolving them are less familiar, and there is more uncertainty about women's roles and their effects. Most respondents, on the whole, still see women as a potentially positive force in politics although the women who have been closer to political activities are less likely to believe that there will be any great differences in American society if women gain political power.

Most active women are convinced that a woman could become President of the United States and even express a willingness to vote for a woman Presidential candidate but, paradoxically, a good many feel distressed about what it would mean if a woman were elected to that office. The anger they have felt at being ignored in their communities, an anger that contributed to their becoming involved in the activities of the assertive community organizations, has not moved them to become particularly supportive of the idea of women's holding higher political offices. Rather, they are troubled about the breakdown in sex roles which such a turn of events would entail. Even more strongly, the active women voice distress about any movement away from traditional family roles.

Although the active women do not in any way connect their community activities to the wider social movement for women's liberation, they are obviously acting in ways which are precisely those advocated by the ideology of the movement: exercising options to get involved in activities outside the family and entering arenas of power

previously reserved for men.   And they are experiencing the effects which the ideology of the
movement could have predicted.   They feel a
greater   sense   of   personal   competence   and
stronger self-esteem, but, in the process, they
are beginning to experience some conflict about
their role commitments.

[VII]

Political Correlates
of Organizational Participation

If there is one message that comes through strongly and consistently in the literature on American women and politics it is that women, compared to men, have historically been less involved in the political process. On virtually any measure of participation or activism, women are shown to be less political: they have, over the years, been less likely to vote, less likely to work for candidates, and considerably less likely to run for political office.[1] They have been found, as well, to have "a lower sense of political involvement, a lower sense of political efficacy, and to be less sophisticated with respect to political conceptualization than men."[2]

The most lucid argument for why these differences exist is that which explicates the sex-specific ways in which males and females are socialized into political roles. Lynne B. Iglitzin, examining the issue from an historical perspective, looks at the ways in which boys and girls in our society have been prepared for political roles and comments on how the actual practice has deviated from the democratic ideal:

If the ideal citizen was expected to be independent, informed, knowledgeable, politically concerned, and aware--and if existing patterns of socialization did not fully succeed in inculcating these traits in boys and men--how much more difficult, if not impossible,

159

> was it to instill them in women, who were taught
> almost from birth to be dependent, submissive, con-
> cerned only with the private, domestic things of
> life.[3]

Iglitzin speaks in the past tense, but if the
verbs were changed to reflect the present the
analysis would remain an accurate one.

The picture of apolitical woman, then, has
been a popular and persistent one. But there
was never an expectation of such apolitical behavior for the active women of the Southwest
Side. There are two reasons for this. First,
the historical trend in general is changing.
Recent studies are beginning to show less evidence of differences between the sexes, at least
in some areas of political behavior such as
voting.[4] Women, after all, were denied the
vote, the most fundamental tool necessary for
access to the political system, until 1920.
Little wonder that in the decades immediately
after that they were less active and sophisticated vis-a-vis the political system than their
husbands and fathers who had always "handled
political things" for the family. Now women
appear to be catching up, although in some areas
such as running for state and national office
progress is slow and women continue to be dis-
proportionately excluded.

Secondly, these women as a group could be
expected to be more politicized than the general
population because they have been selected on
the basis of a concern about community problems
and a commitment to the resolution of those
problems. Women with such an orientation and
concern, which is clearly a political one, can
be expected to evidence interest and activity in
other political areas as well--and they do.

Unfortunately, no direct data were col-
lected on the attitudes and behaviors of men
from the Southwest Side, so it is not possible
here to compare political responses by sex.
Comparisons can of course be made between those
women in the sample who are involved in
assertive community organizations and those who

are not. The latter group, not having the personal concerns and structural supports requisite to becoming active in assertive community organizations, were expected to show less
involvement in other political activities as
well--and they do.

It was earlier noted that the Southwest
Side, despite its long-standing reputation as a
bastion of the city's Democratic organization,
had recently been evidencing independent political stirrings. In such a political climate,
what are the party alignments of the respondents? Does the traditional Democratic loyalty
beat out the nascent political independence?

Not for the active women. Some 60 percent
claim themselves to be independent of either
political party (see Table 17). About 30 percent claim they are Democrats and only 9 percent
are Republicans. These active women clearly
value their political independence. This is not
surprising, given the fact that they have joined
organizations outside the political mainstream
in order to push for things they could not realize through traditional political channels.

Somewhat more surprisingly, there is also
strong support for an independent position among
the inactive women: 43 percent claim affiliation with neither party. An equal number are
Democrats and 14 percent are Republicans. The
absence of party affiliation here may reflect,
as Verba and Nie suggest it often does, an
avoidance of conflict on the part of the inactive women, an unwillingness to take one side
or the other.[5] It is both feasible and fair,
though, to recognize that sentiments of independence may indicate for the inactive women
just what they do for the active--feelings of
dissatisfaction with and alienation from the
major parties.[6]

Declarations of political independence are
frequently accompanied by a certain self-
consciousness about the changes which have
brought about the abandonment of party affilia-
tions. Some see their independence as ·a break

with family tradition: "I was brought up and
everyone was Catholic, Democratic, and Irish,
and I feel we were brought up with the idea that
you always voted for a Democrat whether he was
good, bad, or anything.   And I've certainly
changed my mind about that."   Others see themselves as part of a broader shift in the
national political mood: "I'm not so cut and
dried, one-sided, as I used to be.   I deviate
more often.   I think we're all more choosy than
we used to be."

Table 17

Political Party Preference of Women and Their
Husbands, by Activity Group

Group	Democrat		Republican		Inde-pendent		Total	
	Per-cent	N	Per-cent	N	Per-cent	N	Per-cent	N
Active women	32	7	9	2	60	13	101	22
Husbands of active women	38	7	6	1	55	10	99	19
Inactive women	43	6	14	2	43	6	100	14
Husbands of inactive women	71	10	14	2	14	2	99	14

Over the years, political science and popular wisdom accepted with little question the
idea that men provide political leadership for
women in the family and in the community.   For
example, it is often noted that husbands and
wives have similar party loyalties and vote for
the same candidates.   This has usually been explained in terms of male political influence.
"Men are expected to be dominant in action
directed toward the world outside the family,"
says Levitt.   "Women are to accept that leadership passively."[7] It could as well be explained

as one of the respondents did: "I think it's
strictly because, ah, being a family, I guess
they think alike and they probably discuss this
sort of thing and they come to the same conclusions for the same reasons."

The women were asked about their husbands'
party preferences in order to see the extent to
which there is agreement between the couples on
this dimension.   The husbands of active women
pretty much follow the same pattern as their
wives, at least according to their wives' perceptions.   A majority of the husbands of active
women are independent of both political parties
(see Table 17).   The husbands of the inactive
women, however, are overwhelmingly perceived by
their wives as Democrats: 71 percent place
their husbands in that category.   As noted
earlier, the husbands of inactive women are less
educated than either their own wives or the
active women and men.   Possibly the need to
obtain a job and other political favors through
the workings of the Democratic machine is more
pressing for people with fewer resources and,
consequently, party loyalty is more readily sum-
moned.   In any case, only 14 percent of the inactive   women   have   politically   independent
husbands.

There is not much inter-couple difference
in party preference among these respondents.
Wherever information exists on both spouses,
their choices were matched. Among couples where
the wife is active, only three of eighteen
couples are in disagreement, giving then an 83
percent agreement rate.   Among the inactive
couples, four of the fourteen are in disagreement, giving them a somewhat lower agreement
rate of 71 percent.

A perfectly reasonable explanation for the
high rate of agreement among the women and their
husbands is that offered above by one woman:
family members discuss important political
issues and arrive at a shared position. This is
especially likely to be the case among the
families of active women because membership in

an assertive community organization implies
that political issues are salient for the wives,
and the high rate of joint memberships suggests
the same for the husbands.

The women were asked how often they and
their husbands discuss political issues.   A
majority of the active women respond that they
and their husbands talk about politics "frequently" or "sometimes" (see Table 18).   There
is little difference between the two active
groups on this: 72 percent of the very active
and 67 percent of the somewhat active women
spend at least some time discussing politics at
home. A majority of the inactive women, on the
other hand, "rarely" or "never" discuss politics
with their husbands. One inactive woman says
simply, "I don't like politics. I don't like to
discuss it.   I'd just rather stay out of it."
Another shows more interest in such issues herself but sees her husband as uninterested: "My
husband, he doesn't talk about out-of-the-way
things, like it's not normal for him to sit down
and talk about the President, you know. When
the Democratic convention came on television,
I was very involved with it and I wanted to see
it, but I was afraid he'd want to watch a ball
game. . . ."

Table 18

Responses to: "How Often Do You and Your Husband
Discuss Politics?" by Activity Group

Group	Frequently/ Sometimes		Rarely/Never		Total	
	Per- cent	N	Per- cent	N	Per- cent	N
Very active women	72	8	27	3	99	11
Somewhat active women	67	4	33	2	100	6
Inactive women	44	4	55	5	99	9

These results lend support to the suggestion that the high rate of inter-couple agreement between active women and their husbands is a result of political discussion and consensus within the family. Politics are discussed often in the homes of active women, both spouses often take positions independent of the political parties, and there is a high level of agreement on political identification between them.

While the respondents express a strong desire to maintain independence of either political party, this does not curtail their participation in the political system where affiliation with a particular party, candidate, or issue is called for. Behaviors such as voting, working for a candidate in a political campaign, participating in a public demonstration, and attending meetings on issues of community concern are participatory activities which demand that a citizen take a stand.

The most fundamental act of political participation in a democracy is voting, and the women on the Southwest Side of Chicago--at least those in this sample--do vote. Over 90 percent of the respondents claim to have voted in the 1968 Presidential election; this is about a 20 percent higher voting rate than is found in the general population.[8]

Voting is a specific case where the issue of husbands' influence emerges, and a specific area where political scientists have claimed that women follow their husbands' leads. Campbell and his colleagues, for example, found 27 percent of their sample of married women "admitting that their husbands' opinions helped them decide on their voting choices, as contrasted with only 6 percent of the married men voters admitting influence by their wives."[9]

Whether or not women vote as their husbands do was discussed with several women. One woman who is not active in an assertive community organization admittedly eschews any interest in politics and willingly follows her husband's suggestions.

> I vote with my husband, cause [women] are not in-
> terested in politics. We're so concentrated on kids
> and housework and trying to make a buck stretch that
> that's kind of out of our line.

A number of the inactive women admit they might
be influenced by their husbands because "husbands tend to keep up with political issues more
than women and if they think anywhere alike they
would respect the position of their husbands."

The active women who discussed this, however, paint no such picture of their family interaction. While there may be similarity in the
voting behavior of husband and wife it is seen
to be because "both of you in a discussion discuss the people and come to a conclusion. You
influence each other and that's why you both
vote for the same people." In some families,
the process of political influence may actually
be operating in the opposite direction, as one
respondent speculates: "I wonder if it isn't
changing with the scale going the other way,
with women being more active and more informed
. . . they can bring home, to the dinner table,
a lot of information that can shape their husbands' opinions and the way they vote."

The information obtained on this issue is
sketchy, but it suggests that women who are
active in assertive community organizations are
not about to abandon their political franchise
by casting their votes on the basis of their
husbands' suggestions alone. They value their
political independence too much for that. The
inactive women, on the other hand, do not appear
to mind letting their husbands do the political
thinking for them. They care less about politics and its issues and are content to let the
men handle political questions.

Working for a political candidate is a
political act engaged in far less frequently
than voting by the American populace; only about
one-quarter of the national population has ever
worked for a party or candidate during an election campaign.[10] Campaigning requires more
time, more effort, and more commitment to a

always, however, support is qualified: the demonstration must be nonviolent to be acceptable.

In the beginning, I thought demonstrations were very,
very strange. I could never have participated in
anything like that when I was a kid. That would have
been taboo, forget it. But now I seem to think that
things are happening. If they're peaceful and they
really believe in what they're doing, I think it's a
fine thing. But I have never done it myself. Maybe
someday I will but as yet I haven't.

Demonstrations are acknowledged to be
effective mechanisms for voicing complaints.
But their very necessity is viewed by many as
regrettable.

I think they stink. The way the people are treated on
television, the way it's presented. A group of
mothers grabbing their kids picketed the school or
whatever. They're not treated with respect, that
what they said made sense. But I don't know how else
to do it. You could write a letter and they'd throw
it away and at least by getting it that way you might
get some news company, or be on television, and get it
known to other people how you feel, and you're
trying.

With few exceptions, the women see mass-
based demonstrations as essential. What, after
all, are the alternatives? "If you just tell
people sincerely what you want, they'll listen,"
says one inactive women. But none of the women
who have attempted to change things in their
neighborhoods share her optimistic view.

The overall attitude toward public demonstrations, then, is one of ambivalence. The
women are not comfortable with either the practice or the idea of demonstrations; yet they are
strong supporters of such assertive tactics for
pragmatic reasons.

In a Catholic community, the participation
of priests and nuns in public demonstrations is
often controversial and a factor that adds to
the uncomfortable feelings about demonstrations. Not unexpectedly, this topic arouses
strong opinions on the Southwest Side. Like

other Catholics, adults here are confused by
some of the changes occurring in their church,
and one of the changes that has been both highly
visible and confusing is the new role of political activist which has been assumed by many
priests. Two of the community organizations
have priests as their leading figures. One of
the priests is in questionable standing with his
church because of the racism alleged to be present in the preaching and organizing he has done
to keep white people in his community. The other
focuses on issues of pollution and taxation and
is perceived in the community as a liberal. The
political and social philosophies of these two
priests, as well as the concerns around which
they have organized, differ greatly. Yet both
frequently organize and join in public
demonstrations--both symbolize for the community the new political role of the clergy.

The Catholic women of the community have
responded in different ways to their priests'
becoming political. One woman harbors such
strong opposition to this turn of events that
she has stopped going to services at her church
altogether. Another woman, however, refers to
herself as a "come-backer," one who had stopped
going to church and is now attending again because she agrees so thoroughly with what the
activist priest at her church has to say. A
majority of women support the idea of priests'
participating in public demonstrations. They
see it as a priest's right and, some add, a
priest's duty.

Perhaps it is because residents have models
of activist priests close at hand that they find
it easy to voice support for this kind of behavior. In any case, a majority do, and, not
surprisingly, the active women more than their
inactive neighbors favor priests' assuming such
a role. The very active women have a tendency
to go beyond mere support and claim it is a
priest's duty to take part in solving the problems of the community. Sometimes this is
phrased in terms of the community's need for the
leadership that priests can provide: "They're

the only ones with the influence who are socially aware."

One active woman, anger in her voice, tells how she feels about priests' getting involved:

> I think it's very good. I think it's about time. The church has always kind of been the one people agree with and [if] some of these priests get off their duffs instead of sit around their rectory in their little glorified castle and get out and work for the community, a lot more people would come out. . . . Get out and work with the people. That's where it all is. That's where the church is. The church is not inside of the church that you go to once a week.

The inactive women are less sure. About half favor priests' participating in demonstration if they want to, but the other half are decidedly against such behavior or, at best, ambivalent. Those who oppose priests' participating tend to base their opposition on the loss of respect which they believe a priest undergoes when he moves from dealing with the affairs of God to dealing with the affairs of the world.

> I don't like it one bit. I don't think they have any part in it, any business. The church shouldn't get involved. I think that's why the nuns lost their respect, when you see them walking and changing habits and all. I don't think they have any business doing that.

Those who have chosen to participate in demonstrations themselves are far more willing to concede to their clergy a comparable right. Indeed, the most active women are eager to share the burdens. Those who have not themselves engaged in such behavior are not so enthusiastic.

One final measure of political participation was sought from the inactive women: whether or not they had attended any community meetings dealing with local problems in the last two years. For the active women, of course, attendance at such meetings is built into the very definition of being active. Women who do not actually belong to a community organization

might still attend neighborhood meetings where
local problems are discussed. As it turns out,
a majority had not, although some had. Twenty-
seven percent had attended one or two community
meetings in the preceding few years; 13 percent
had attended more than that. Most of these
meetings focused on discussions of local problems, such as drug use among teen-agers, and
were sponsored by a local church or school.

One inactive woman who had not attended any
meetings typifies the person who sees politics
not only as uninteresting, but also as a purely
private affair:

> No, I don't get involved too deeply in that. There's
> a lot of bickering going on in that. They all say the
> Republicans are no good, the Democrats are no good,
> and they all fight. So it's best to keep quiet and
> believe what you want to believe and do what you want
> to do.

An organizationally active woman, who
attends meetings constantly and is obviously
stimulated by the excitement of the political
world, expresses disdain for the kind of woman
depicted above who disallows the public nature
of politics. "I really have no patience," she
says. "I'm not involved, they say. But you are
involved. These people are making laws that you
have to live by. They have involved you. Once
you're born, you're involved, whether you want
to be or not."

Participation in political events such as
campaign activities, public demonstrations, and
community meetings is built on some knowledge of
the politcal system and some interest in its
workings. Both these qualities, at least at a
minimal level, must of necessity precede political participation. Not surprisingly, then, the
active women come out far ahead on indicators of
political knowledge and political interest.

Knowing the name of one's alderman is a
simple but straightforward measure of political
knowledge at the local level. The alderman is
the local ward's representative to the City
Council and his office is the one through which

citizens channel local complaints or requests. All but one of the active women know who their alderman is. Among the inactive women, on the other hand, almost half do not know the name of their alderman. The active woman, of course, deals with her alderman in the course of her organizational activities and has thus come to know him.

It is of interest here, as well as indicative of the nature of Chicago politics, that several of the inactive women who could not name their aldermen did know the name of their precinct captains and volunteered that information. The Democratic organization in Chicago has traditionally thrived on having highly effective personal contacts between Democratic precinct captains and the residents of a precinct, which is a geographic area substantially smaller than an alderman's ward. In any case, information about precinct captains was not solicited.

As with political knowledge, there are a number of ways in which interest in the political system can be gauged. The extent to which one follows political events in newspapers and magazines is one; discussing political issues with friends and family is another. One particular aspect of the latter measure, the extent to which the women and their husbands talk together about political issues, was discussed earlier; the active women emerged as frequently involved in such discussions.

High levels of political involvement have traditionally been found to parallel strong feelings of political efficacy, i.e., "the feeling that individual political action does have, or can have, an impact upon the political process."[13] Such a correlation exists with obvious good reason; individuals who believe that their actions can make a difference in the workings of the political system will be the ones who engage in those actions. Males, the college-educated, those with high incomes, and those whose occupations are accorded a high status are the ones who have generally been

found to hold such feelings of efficacy,[14] and
they are the ones who have participated most
extensively in political activites. They are
also the ones who are more likely to be in
positions of power and influence and are objec-
tively most able to make the political system
respond to their wishes.

The respondents, being females who are not
college educated and who live with men whose
jobs pay modest salaries and have low status,
might be expected to score low on any measure of
political efficacy. Their social position,
after all, is not one which has carried much
weight in American politics. On the other hand,
one sub-group of the sample, the very active
women, participates in political activities
more vigorously than either their neighbors or
the population as a whole. And the fact that
the very active women are consideraly more convinced than the other women that people "like
them" can resolve local problems leads to the
expectation that this group will emerge with
feelings of efficacy stronger than those of the
less active and inactive women.

The respondents were asked three questions
which have long been used to tap feelings of
efficacy. The results do not consistently work
in the predicted direction, but the inconsisten-
cies may reflect the peculiar relationship which
Americans had with their political system in
1972 as much as it does any ambivalent feelings
on the part of the women. The cumulative revelations of manipulation and deception on the
part of public officials have made these items
as much a measure of accurate perception as of
political efficacy.

The first item presented to respondents
was: "How much political power do people like
you have--none, not very much, some, or a great
deal?" The results here are strikingly in the
expected direction, as Table 21 shows. Seventy
percent of the very active women believe that
they have at least some political power. The
less active and the inactive women are in the
opposite camp, with 100 percent and 67 percent

respectively believing they have not very much
power or none at all.

Women who have attempted to exert some influence on the political structure view themselves as having greater power than those who
have not done so at all or who, as in the case of
the somewhat actives, have not done so to as
great an extent. Again, it is not simply organizational membership, but the nature and extent
of participation in the organization that makes
the difference.

Table 21

Responses to: "How Much Political Power Do People
Like You Have?" by Activity Group

Group	Much[a]		Little[b]	
	Per-cent	N	Per-cent	N
Very active women	70	7	30	3
Somewhat active women	--		100	5
Inactive women	33	4	67	8

[a]"Some" or "A great deal."

[b]"Not very much" or "None."

Most of the very active women who say they
are possessors of much power view that power in
potential terms. It will become a real power
only if people "get together." The following
qualification is typical: "If people would get
together on issues that affect them and vote in
a block, then we'd probably have a lot of
power." One woman directly expresses the effect
her organizational activity has had on her
feelings about political power: "People together, you can have a lot, you can really do
the job. I'd have never believed it two years

ago." Those few inactive women who claim that "people like them" have a great deal of power do not add such qualifying statements.

Respondents were then asked to agree or disagree with the statement, "People like me don't have any say about what the government does." Here, a majority of the very active women assume the position traditionally labeled non-efficacious: they agree that people like them do not have any say in the government (see Table 22). Fewer of the somewhat active and the inactive women agree. In other words, those women who have in fact most often made their views known to the government are the ones most likely to believe they have no say in what the government does, while the women who have not been active in any assertive politically-oriented community organization are more likely to deny that they lack a say in the government. Those who have been least active most vehemently deny it: 40 percent of the inactive women dis-agree strongly.

Table 22

Responses to: "People Like Me Don't Have Any Say in What the Government Does," by Activity Group

Group	Agree Strongly		Agree Somewhat		Disagree Somewhat		Disagree Strongly	
	Per-cent	N	Per-cent	N	Per-cent	N	Per-cent	N
Very active women	7	1	50	7	21	3	21	3
Somewhat active women	17	1	17	1	50	3	17	1
Inactive women	13	2	27	4	20	3	40	6

Responses to this item would seem to indicate that women who have attempted to make the government responsive to their demands have learned that such a task is, at best, difficult.

They have also learned through experience that
government officials will often do as they like
regardless of what most people say or want. The
inactive women, less involved in all phases of
politics, appear to accept from an untested
position the idea that everyone has a say in
what the government does. Is it legitimate to
say, according to responses to this item, that
the inactive women feel more efficacious politically? Perhaps so, but that appears to be a
feeling based on little contact or concern with
the political system. The active women likely
have a clearer picture of the ways in which they
are excluded from decisions about what the
government does.

Varying perceptions of just what it is that
the government is doing may also be reflected
here. The active women, as evidenced by their
organizational participation, have grievances.
They see their government doing things they do
not like. The inactive women may not see the
government operating against their interests;
it may be recalled that they did not see as many
problems in their neighborhoods. If they are
less likely to see a discrepancy between what
the government provides and what they would
like, it follows that they would be less likely
to feel they are not being heard.

Despite the fact that they are more likely
than the others to believe they have no say in
what the government does, the active women turn
out to be most likely to feel they understand
what is going on in the political world. Still,
a majority of them, as of the other two groups,
agrees with the statement, "Sometimes politics
and government seem so complicated that a person
like me can't really understand what's going
on." Fifty-seven percent of the very active
women agree (see Table 23). A greater percentage of the somewhat actives and almost three-
fourths of the inactives do not understand what
is going on in politics. Given the constant
expansion of governmental bureaucracies,
regulations, and complexities, it appears quite
reasonable for a majority of respondents to see

the government as sometimes too complicated for
their comprehension. But the more one has been
involved in the working of the political system
the less likely one is to be overwhelmed by
those complexities.

Table 23

Responses to: "Sometimes Politics and Government Seem
So Complicated That a Person Like Me Can't Really
Understand What's Going On," by Activity Group

Group	Agree Strongly		Agree Somewhat		Disagree Somewhat		Disagree Strongly	
	Per-cent	N	Per-cent	N	Per-cent	N	Per-cent	N
Very active women	14	2	43	6	7	1	36	5
Somewhat active women	17	1	50	3	17	1	17	1
Inactive women	27	4	47	7	13	2	13	2

Responses to these measures of political
efficacy suggest that activity in an assertive
community organization has a complex effect on
women's feelings vis-a-vis the political
system. Those women who are very active in the
organizations overwhelmingly agree that they
have a good deal of potential political power if
only they could come together and realize it.
At the same time, a majority feel they do not
presently have any say in what the government
does. For this group of women, such an apparent
contradiction makes perfect sense. The reason
they are forming and joining assertive community
organizations is to find, within the political
system, a voice that they feel they are lacking
now; if they can ever get their group sufficiently well organized and supported, they will
finally have some political power. While a
majority of this group do acknowledge that the
complexities of the government and political
system make it hard sometimes for them to under-

stand what is going on, they are less inclined
to say this than the other women. It seems
plausible that, as a result of their activities,
the political system is now less difficult to
comprehend than it once was.

The inactive women are more likely to find
the workings of government complicated and considerably less likely to believe that people
like them have much political power; yet they
will not accept the notion that they do not have
a say in what the government does. Such an
acknowledgment apparently constitutes a more
basic criticism of the workings of the American
system than they care to make. It might also
put them in an incongruous position--if they
felt they had no say in the government, they
might have to defend their lack of attempts to
gain a voice. Nevertheless, a contradiction
persists when the inactive women admit they have
no power but will not admit they have no say in
the government.

The somewhat active women, once again, are
in the middle: they are most cynical about the
political power they hold, most optimistic about
the say in government that people like them
have, and in the middle in terms of how complicated they view government and politics to be.

The lack of any clear or consistent pattern
makes it difficult to speculate on what these
results mean. Once again, it appears that membership that is merely nominal has little impact
on political behavior or attitudes--in this
case, feelings of efficacy--while intensive involvement in an assertive community organization correlates with what may be judged a
realistic assessment of minimal input into the
political system as things are currently operating combined with a strong sense of potential
power and a diminishing befuddlement with the
complexities of government.

The fact that the women were interviewed
only once makes it difficult to determine if
differences which are evident between the active
and the inactive respondents are the results of

or the precedents of organizational participation.   This is a question which persists
throughout this analysis.   It may be safe to
assume that participation in demonstrations
follows joining assertive community organizations and, more tentatively, one could make the
same assumption about participation in campaign
activities. But it is impossible to speak with
certainty about the origin of feelings and attitudes toward the political system.   Does the
feeling that they have little say in the government, for example, spur women to become involved
or is it a feeling which grows more intense as
more time is spent in an assertive community
organization?

        While the issue of causality must persist
in an unresolved fashion, this does not preclude
some speculation about which attitudes are results of participation.   Such speculation can
proceed with some legitimacy when the respondents themselves corroborate that these attitudes do indeed constitute changes for them.

        Most of the active women admit to having
been changed--politically and otherwise--by
their organizational experiences. The most frequently mentioned political change is an increased awareness of how the political system
and public officials really operate. "Your eyes
are opened," says one woman.

> I think they [public officials] think we're all very
> stupid and we don't know what's going on. . . . They
> just automatically assume we're ignorant. And they
> can make a blank [sic] statement and you have to
> contradict them. Awareness. That's the thing that
> [the organization] has given us, awareness.

        The community organizations in which these
women are active engage in a good deal of
investigatory and research work--looking up
laws, tracking down owners of buildings, finding
tax assessment records, compiling statistics on
schools and air pollutants. Members must be
prepared to back their organizations' demands
with facts and figures. Once they are prepared
and confront their protagonists, they often

encounter an appalling ignorance or lack of concern on the part of public officials. This,
along with the facts they have uncovered, has
fueled the anger of the participants.

> I was always aware of the evils, if you want to use
> the word, but I've learned so much more in the past
> two years and the more I learn the madder I get .
> . . . It teaches you a great deal about the mechanics
> of government, and it makes you sick.

The increased knowledge and awareness to
which so many organizational members refer may
well explain why the very active women were less
likely to agree that government and politics are
so complicated that they cannot understand what
is going on. They are beginning to understand
what is going on, not only through their own
research but because, as many mention, being involved in community activities whets one's
appetite for learning more. The active women
find themselves reading newspapers more often
and more thoroughly and generally keeping up
with what is going on in a way they had not done
previously.

With their heightened awareness of how the
political system operates, the women find themselves not only more angry but also more able to
break through the mystique which for them had
surrounded corporate and political figures.
Gradually, these public figures have become not
only ordinary persons but in many cases men who
are no longer perceived as very intelligent or
competent. One woman expresses how this realization influenced her:

> Another thing I've found out, and I don't mean this in
> an egotistical way at all, but they're not very smart
> people. I always thought [politicians and corporate
> officials] were probably very shrewd, very wise, had
> minds like computers--and they don't. And that came
> to me as kind of a shock and it helped my ego and I
> wasn't afraid to fight them. They're just ordinary
> human beings. They're not very bright at all. . . .
> You don't have to fear them at all as far as your mind
> being able to cope with their mind, not at all. And
> that helps you.

Increased knowledge, along with a reduc-
tion in respect for public officials, might be
expected to lead to increased cynicism with
respect to the political system. And cynicism
is evident, but not as widespread as might be
predicted. Respondents were asked if they
agreed or disagreed with the following statement: "Public officials are really only interested in people's votes and not in their
opinions." Two-thirds of the respondents take
the more cynical position and agree with this
statement, as Table 24 shows. But the most
cynical group is not the active women whom we
would expect to be more aware of the venality of
public officials, but the inactive women, 80
percent of whom express the belief that public
officials are not interested in their opinions.
In contrast, 64 percent of the very active and
one-third of the somewhat active women are in
agreement. This may provide further rationale
for why the inactive women are not motivated to
join the local assertive community organiza-
tions--so far as they are concerned, raising
their voices would not make any difference.

Table 24

Responses to: "Public Officials Are Really Only
Interested in People's Votes and Not in Their
Opinions," by Activity Group

Group	Agree Strongly		Agree Somewhat		Disagree Somewhat		Disagree Strongly	
	Per- cent	N	Per- cent	N	Per- cent	N	Per- cent	N
Very active women	21	3	43	6	29	4	7	1
Somewhat active women	--		33	2	67	4	--	
Inactive women	20	3	60	9	7	1	13	2

These results also suggest that active

women--who admittedly may have been less cynical all along--are experiencing a decrease in cynicism as they become more aware of the ways in which they can make public officials listen and react to their opinions. By and large, the assertive community organizations have not been effective enough for long enough to develop an impressive track record for gaining concessions from public officials, but they certainly have made themselves heard. And that may be enough for participants to believe that they are able to make their opinions a matter of interest to public officials. A conviction that their opinions and not just their votes are sought also helps explain why the active women are more willing than the inactive to engage in public demonstrations and campaign activities--these are other ways of making their opinions heard-- and, further, why they are more inclined to believe that people like them do have political power when they operate collectively.

This chapter suggests ways in which membership in an assertive community organization is related to other political attitudes and measures of political participation. There is strong evidence that those who are very active in an assertive community organization are more likely to be engaged in the political activities of campaigning and demonstrating. They are also more likely to claim political independence and more likely to view politics as an issue worth discussing at home. On two of three measures of political efficacy they score stronger than the inactive women; they are more likely to believe people like them have power and less likely to find workings of the governmental and political system so complicated that they cannot understand it. They emerge as less efficacious on the third measure: they are less inclined to believe they have a say in what the government does. Finally, the most active women are less cynical than their inactive neighbors; they more often believe government officials are interested in their opinions.

The somewhat active women, more than the

inactives but less than the very actives, discuss politics with their husbands, participate
in demonstrations, support clergy participation
in demonstrations, and are not confused by
politics. But they are the least likely to have
worked on a political candidate's campaign and
the least likely to believe they have any political power. Where the very active women consistently distinguish themselves from the
inactive and clearly emerge as having a distinct
orientation toward the political system, the
somewhat active women do not. Nominal membership in a community organization, even an assertive one, does not produce a more politicized
citizen in the same way that active membership
does.

    While it remains for future research to
determine with certainty whether membership in
an assertive community organization generates
rather than reflects a politicized perspective,
the evidence presented here argues that it does.
On this basis, it can be expected that this new
role that working-class women are forging for
themselves for a range of reasons--personal,
structural, and political--will, regardless of
individual motivation, tend to have a politicizing effect on its occupants.

[VIII]

The Bases of Division: Race and Social Class

> It depends on the class of the racial group. Like, if a policeman moved in here who was black, I'd be pretty sure he was middle class, but if a woman with seven kids moved in, I'd say how can she raise seven kids without a husband, and the answer would be public aid. That would be different.

There are immediate and pressing concerns which have moved the women of the Southwest Side into action. There are, as well, structural and psychological variables which make the possibility that some women will become active more likely. Another dimension of activism, its ideological underpinnings, began to emerge in the last chapter. Despite limited support for the goals of the women's movement and the absence of an explicitly feminist perspective, the active women were found to be acting in ways and exercising options which ultimately support many of the movement's goals. It remains for this chapter to examine additional crucial aspects of the respondents' ideology. The questions addressed here are: what are the prevailing attitudes toward issues of race and social class and to what extent do these attitudes constitute forces which motivate participation in assertive community organizations?

Racial and social class attitudes are central to this analysis for several reasons.

First, race and social class are traditional groupings around which political ideology develops and political activism emerges. Given this, it is of particular interest to see if the active women have perspectives on racial and class issues which differ in any noticeable ways from those of the inactive women. Secondly, race, as indicated throughout this book, is an overwhelmingly salient issue in this community. The threat of racial change was the impetus for much organizing; problems revolving around racial concerns are identified as the major ones facing the community; there is a pervasive anxiety in the area about the pending need to relocate as blacks move more deeply into previously all-white neighborhoods. All these factors, discussed earlier, are convincing with respect to the centrality of racial concerns, but provide little understanding of what values, priorities, and beliefs underlie the anxiety. Are racial concerns, for example, as the woman quoted at the beginning of the chapter suggests, primarily reflective of social class concerns? Third, with respect to social class itself, there is evidence of a rudimentary class consciousness among the respondents, both active and inactive. There is an overwhelming conviction among the women that people like them, people in their social class, are treated unfairly in this society. From this conviction derives evident anger. But what beyond this are their thoughts about social class and economic inequality? These questions of race and class are explored in this chapter in hopes of arriving at a better understanding of the political consciousness of the women on the Southwest Side of Chicago, both those who have chosen to be active in assertive community organizations and those who have not.

Before moving into any specific discussion of relationships between racial or class groups, the women were asked to respond to a more general question. "A lot of people in the United States today seem to think of themselves as oppressed or kept down by society. Are there any groups that you think are particularly

oppressed or kept down in any way?" The intent
of this question was to see which groups the
women would select on their own, without any
suggestions. Responses naming women, black
Americans, or people like them ("working
people," "average Americans") were particularly
watched for as these, it was thought, might
suggest an awareness of women's oppression,
racism, or class inequities.

As it turned out, only one respondent mentioned women specifically; two others, who
believe everyone is kept down, include women on
their lists. Only 10 percent mention "people
like us." Blacks are the single group most
often named, but less than one-third of the
women make this selection. A number of the
respondents who did not choose blacks went out
of their way to note that blacks were not kept
down any longer. "I think years ago the black
people were, but I think now things have definitely changed for them and if they want to,
they can climb the ladder too." Interestingly,
American Indians were named almost as frequently
as blacks and Latinos were not far behind.

The largest group of respondents, almost
two-fifths of the women, contend that no particular groups of people are oppressed in America.
While they readily admit that a lot of people
have a hard time making it, they do not believe
that there is any systematic discrimination
against particular groups. This position
derives from a perspective which views success
or failure solely in individual terms. Anyone
who is willing to work hard can get ahead. "If
you really want to strive for something you'll
achieve it and it's your own fault if you can't
do it because there are so many opportunities
now, even given to the poor class, the government helps them with education and all."
Another puts it more succinctly: "Anybody can
get out and get a job and work."

Such a perspective, which is strong in this
community, shows little sensitivity to the
institutional racism and other kinds of systematic oppression which become embedded in the

structures of a society. Yet this belief that
individuals can break out of a deprived background and "get ahead" is built on the experience these women, their husbands, their parents
and their grandparents have had.

> Look at it this way . . . during the Depression, my
> parents, they were on relief, and my father . . . he
> just about made ends meet. . . . And they don't own
> their own home today. And yet we all worked ourselves
> up. Every one of my brothers and sisters that are
> married all own their own homes. . . . They worked to
> build themselves up. . . . Any place we've ever
> gotten, we've gotten on our own and I can't under-
> stand why somebody else can't do it.

Such responses come quickly, often bit-
terly. The American dream did come true, in
some ways at least, for this generation through
the hard work and sacrifices of their parents
and grandparents. Mostly this was achieved
through individual struggle--although it is
often overlooked that the collective struggle
for union-enforced working conditions and wages
made it possible to save some money and begin to
get ahead. What these women resent is not that
a black man or woman or a Latino man or woman
might also get ahead--opportunities are seen as
legitimately extended to everyone. Nor is there
a denial of how much other groups have suffered
and how hard they have worked. Rather, the resentment is that gains are now being made
collectively, by an entire group of people,
rather than on an individual basis. This is not
the way the history they have learned tells them
it was for their families. Furthermore, there
is a strong feeling that the gains of other
groups, like blacks, are being made at the ex-
pense of people like them. One woman complains
that she sees "so many instances where the white
people are just pushed to the rear of the line,
like they say first come, first served, and the
white person comes and he's pushed to the back
and I think that's very unfair."

There are a few people who claim that
everyone is oppressed in some way. "Oh, women,
blacks, Cubans, Indians, Mexicans, men too. I

can't think of anyone actually that isn't used somehow." These women are not able systematically to explicate why they feel most people are treated unfairly; nonetheless they have a vague sense that there is something in the present structure of the society that victimizes or "uses" most citizens.

Somewhat surprisingly, there is no difference in the response patterns of the active and the inactive women. Those who see widespread oppression are a minority. There is an evident reluctance among the respondents to admit to the existence of any systematic oppression as seen by the fact that the single most popular response is the one which denies that anyone suffers from oppression.

The responses to this question are two-edged. Most of the women recognize that inequities have historically been accorded minority groups in this country and that such inequities continue today; still, there is a marked unwillingness to muster up sympathy for others. This appears to be less because they think minority groups are doing well--although they often point to how conditions are improving for these groups--than because they simply do not feel that they, by comparison, are doing much better. One woman, the mother of seven children, who, in the course of the interview, revealed herself to be a person especially sensitive to the problems of others, explains how she feels:

> Well, I have sympathy for the blacks in the ghettos but they seem to be getting some place. Mexican-Americans seem to be getting more aid from the government, as far as scholarships. . . . But I think the middle class is oppressed, the truck driver, the person who saves his money in the bank. In this last truck drivers' strike, if you had any money in the bank . . . you weren't allowed food stamps. Just because we saved, are we being deprived of that aid that Mr. Jones next door didn't put away for himself? Sometimes you wonder.

Working-class families like those on the

Southwest Side have seen the demise of many of
their American ideals.   The scandals of the
Nixon administration at the Federal level and
the Daley machine at the local level have raised
fundamental questions about the systems of politics and justice. The realization that America
lost a war in Southeast Asia and, furthermore,
should never have been there in the first place
raises doubts about government credibility,
special interest groups, and the meaning of
patriotism.   The economic problems of the 1970s
puts comfortable living and job security out of
the reach of increasing numbers of families.

    As these sources of physical and psycho-
logical oppression begin to confront the members
of the white working class and lower middle
class, there are two directions which a response
could take.   People could begin to see the com-
monality of these problems and those of other
groups and then, perhaps, begin to work together
to change things.   In some inchoate way, those
few women who say everyone is oppressed may be
starting to take such a perspective.   The second
possibility is that people so victimized may
become   increasingly   hostile   toward   other
victims, not only because they are seen as sometimes better organized and thus able to take
some small slice of the pie (jobs, houses, university seats) away from them, but also because
other oppressed groups are routinely portrayed
as the "natural" competitors.   The struggle, for
example, is seen to revolve around who gets the
existing jobs rather than around creating more
jobs so everyone can work.   The emphasis on individual struggle, accompanied by the resentful
comments we often heard, suggests that it is
this latter perspective that is more often taken
by the women.

    To see if such an interpretation holds up
when attitudes toward blacks and integration are
probed directly, the women were asked a series
of questions which together comprise a pro-
integration scale in use for over thirty years
by researchers at the National Opinion Research
Center.   This scale was chosen so the responses

of this sample of white, urban women could be compared to the responses of a national sample questioned at roughly the same point in time.[1] The items which make up the scale, the responses of both the active women and the inactive women, and the responses of the general population on the national survey are found in Table 25.

The first item reads, "Do you think white students and black students should go to the same schools, or to separate schools?" In the national survey, 73 percent gave the pro-integration response, supporting black and white children's going to school together. The percentage of women in this sample who give this response is higher: 94 percent of the active women and 84 percent of the inactive women ver-bally support integrated schools. It is essen-tial to note, however, that almost half of the Southwest Side women who indicate such support qualify their responses: "I think they should be in the same schools. If we're gonna live with them and work with them, going to school with them is part of the natural process. I just hate to see this forcing of busloads of them. It makes for a feeling in the school that's wrong. I don't think it's good to force them." Another woman phrases her qualification in social class terms: "I would say they should go to the same schools if they're on the same economic level, but I don't think any-thing should really be forced. If it's on an economic level, it will happen naturally." At least on a verbal level these women are not ob-jecting to integration per se so much as to the idea of having something forced on them, or having their neighborhood become a laboratory for government experiments with integration.

Moving away from a discussion of the scale items for a moment, it is appropriate here to look at the responses to another question on school integration which was worded somewhat differently and was raised during another part of the interview. The women were asked: "Do you think the government should see to it that white and black children go to school together,

Table 25

Percent Giving Pro-Integration Sentiments

Item and Pro-Integration Response[a]	Active Women	Inactive Women	National Sample (1970)
1. "Do you think white students and black students should go to the same schools, or to separate schools?" (Same)	94	84	73
2. "How strongly would you object if a member of your family wanted to bring a black friend home to dinner?" (Not at all)	86	69	63
3. "White people have a right to keep blacks out of their neighborhoods if they want to, and blacks should respect that right." (Disagree Slightly or Disagree Strongly)	59	53	50
4. "Do you think there should be laws against marriages between Negroes and whites?" (No)	100	93	49
5. "Blacks shouldn't push themselves where they're not wanted." (Disagree Slightly or Disagree Strongly)	47	47	16

[a]Two items traditionally included as part of the scale, "Generally speaking, do you think there should be separate sections for Negroes in streetcars and buses?" and "Do you think Negroes should have the right to use the same parks, restaurants and hotels as white people?", are not discussed here. In some cases these questions were asked; in many they were not since respondents' earlier remarks showed support for integration to an extent that these questions would be insulting. Nobody who responded took an anti-integration position on these items, which should now be replaced on the scale with items measuring more subtle aspects of racism.

or should the government stay out of that?" As
Table 26 shows, a strong majority of the women
want the government to stay out of the business
of integrating schools; 65 percent of the active
women and 82 percent of the inactive women take
this position.

Table 26

Responses to: "Do You Think the Government Should See
To It That White and Black Children Go to the Same
Schools, or Should the Government Stay Out
of That?" by Activity Group

Category	Active Women		Inactive Women	
	Per-cent	N	Per-cent	N
Yes, the government should see to it	12	2	9	1
Yes, but government role should be limites	24	4	9	1
The government should stay out of it	65	11	82	9
Total	101	17	100	11

One active woman explains her feelings:

That's a very complicated question. I think that
boundaries should not be set purposely to perpetuate
the system of segregation. But I think the answer
there lies in the quality. I don't see any purpose in
transporting children twenty miles. I don't really
see the purpose of that, especially younger children.

Even among the relatively few women who
support the government's taking a role in integrating the schools, there are qualifications:

I would say in the upper, higher education schools,
high schools, college--that the government could well
see that they went to school together. But I do not
think they should make the younger children, when it

involves busing and all that sort of thing. I don't believe in it.

What can be made of the fact that 90 percent of the respondents believe white and black children should attend the same schools, but less than one-third believe the government should take a role in making certain that this happens? These women appear to be saying that they are willing to accept integrated schools if the integration is "natural," that is, not forced on them by the government. It also appears that the respondents do not support the idea of any deliberate policy of segregating schools any more than they support a deliberate policy of integrating schools. With this interpretation in mind, the seemingly contradictory responses to these questions are actually quite consistent.

Moving back to the pro-integration scale, a strong majority gives the pro-integration response to the second item which reads: "How strongly would you object if a member of your family wanted to bring a black friend home to dinner?" Eighty-six percent of the active women and 69 percent of the inactive women say they would "not at all" object. The active women are considerably more liberal than both their inactive neighbors and the national sample on this issue. Most of the women who say they would not object base that attitude on their respect for the judgment of others in their family. "I don't think I'd object. If my daughter thought enough of them, they'd have to be pretty nice and I don't think I'd object. I think I'd try to be understanding." Those who would object often tend to put their objections in terms of what the neighbors would say. The women who are in assertive community organizations are less concerned with what others think of their behavior; this is evident from the very fact that they have become active in groups that are controversial and subject to the criticism of many in the neighborhoods.

Thus far, the absolute level of support for

integration has been high. However, this support begins to decline with the next item,
"White people have a right to keep blacks out of
their neighborhoods if they want to, and blacks
should respect that right. Do you agree or disagree?" There is not much difference between
the activity groups here: 59 percent of the
active women take the pro-integration position
and disagree, while 53 percent of the inactive
women do so. One inactive woman who takes an
anti-integration position explains: "I agree,
and the same thing stands for the black people.
I think each should have the right to sell to
whom you want to. I mean, after all, it's your
property. If you want to sell to a black one,
fine. If you don't, that's your prerogative or
whatever." Most of the women who took the position supporting all-white neighborhoods added
something to the effect that a comparable right
to keep whites out of their neighborhood belongs
to black people. "Anybody has the right to keep
a certain element out of their community" is the
way one woman expresses it. Those, on the other
hand, who disagreed with the statement offered
little elaboration, simply stating they did not
believe anyone had such a right. The Chicago
women, in the throes of dealing with racial
changes in their neighborhoods, are only
slightly more liberal than the national sample
in response to this item.

The fourth item, "Do you think there should
be laws against marriage between Negroes and
whites?" finds virtually no support among the
respondents. Only one woman, an inactive, felt
that such laws should be on the books. Many of
the other women clearly are not supporters of
inter-racial marriages, but neither do they feel
there should be laws prohibiting them. The de-
emphasis on government intervention in people's
lives and the emphasis on the individual and his
or her freedom to make his or her own choices
comes through again. "That's up to the individual," says one. "I wouldn't want to, but if
somebody else does, let 'em go ahead," says
another. The large discrepancy between the
Chicago sample and the national sample includes

the South, where laws prohibiting inter-racial
marriage and support for such laws have traditionally been stronger than in the North.

The last item shows the least amount of
pro-integration sentiment, and both groups of
women look the same here. Agreement or disagreement was sought for the following statement: "Blacks shouldn't push themselves where
they're not wanted." Forty-seven percent of the
women take the pro-integration response and disagree, allowing to blacks the right to assert
themselves physically or psychologically even
if others do not want them to. The remaining 53
percent take an anti-integration position,
agreeing that blacks should not push.

One of the women who disagrees again puts
the emphasis on the individual: "That would
have to be on an individual basis. If a person
has enough courage and desire to do it, I say
fine, let him do it. I, myself, couldn't do it.
I'd rather stay where I was comfortable." Most
of those on the other side, those who do not
want blacks to push, add that "nobody should
push themselves where they're not wanted."
Given the fact that the active women have been
involved in community organizations whose explicit purpose is to push their interests in an
assertive way because they are not heard when
they use more moderate channels, one might
expect to find them supportive of blacks acting
in comparable fashion. They are, however, no
more so than the inactive women. Nonetheless,
the Southwest Side women are considerably more
supportive of black rights on this issue than is
the national sample. Only 16 percent of the
1970 national sample supported the right of
black people to push themselves where they are
not wanted.

The two items on which there is relatively
less pro-integration support lend some tenta-
tive support to the earlier interpretation of
the direction which the frustration of white
working-class women might be taking. Agreement
with the item which claims white people have a
right to keep blacks out of their neighborhoods

suggests that blacks are seen as competitors for limited resources--in this case decent houses and neighborhoods. Many whites, with a certain amount of historical backing, believe that if blacks gain homes in a neighborhood, they will lose them. Certainly the women on the Southwest Side feel this very strongly. The other item on which integration support is low--"Blacks should not push themselves where they're not wanted"--shows, at least implicitly, a resentment toward the fact that blacks have, with collective strength, been making demands on the institutions of society and winning some concessions. The hostility toward blacks is built at least partly around anger at another group's collectively getting or threatening to get some of those very things for which these women and their families struggled on an individual basis and now are in danger of losing.

Even as some explanation is developed for the evident anti-black sentiments, it must be emphasized that there is little support in these data for the stereotyped image of the working-class racist. While there are some elements of racism among some of these women, they are considerably fewer than what is found among other groups of Americans. Comparison with the national sample shows this. Indeed, these women are struggling daily with questions of integration in their neighborhoods and schools; their struggle has an immediacy few other Americans share.

On one item on the pro-integration scale-- the one dealing with blacks pushing themselves-- there is no difference in attitude between the active women and their inactive neighbors. On the remaining four items the active women emerge as stronger supporters of integration than the inactive, although the differences between the activity groups are seldom great.

Very few of these women espouse all-white neighborhoods. In the course of the discussion about integration, respondents mentioned what they felt would be the ideal ratio of blacks to whites in their neighborhoods. Only two of the active women expressed preference for an all-white neighborhood. Most chose somewhere between 10 and 25 percent black as ideal; a few thought more than one-quarter but less than one-half black would be ideal. The inactive women were twice as likely to prefer an all-white neighborhood and twice as likely to be unable to answer the question.

Almost invariably the women believe that if the percentage of black families in the neighborhood should go over what they see as ideal "the white people would panic, because they're in the minority and they would leave, and in no time at all it becomes all black." No one among these women wants to live in a neighborhood where whites are a minority; several recognize this themselves. "I don't really feel I have any prejudice against blacks, but I wouldn't want to be in the minority," says one who then goes on to explain that she doesn't "like to be in the minority of anything." No one raises the question of how black people feel being in the minority. An integrated neighborhood invariably means a neighborhood with a minority of blacks. A neighborhood which is 10 percent black is considered integrated. A neighborhood which is 10 percent white is not considered integrated but, as several women put it, "resegregated."

One inactive woman proposed a unique solution to the question of neighborhood integration: "I've always felt they should divide the city," she explains. "Then, maybe white people could have certain boundaries and colored would have certain boundaries." This same woman, in discussing social classes, felt "rich people should not mingle with working people." This woman is an extreme example of a tendency observed in far more modified ways among other respondents: an implicit desire to preserve a kind of social order where distinctions and demarcations between groups of people are clear and generally acknowledged. This vision of the social order is more vividly revealed when respondents talk about social classes.

Another conclusion drawn from these responses and the accompanying comments is one which was alluded to earlier: these women desire a minimum amount of government intervention in their community and in their lives in general. Such a conclusion is supported both by the results on the two integrated school items which were discussed above and by the results on the NORC item about interracial marriages. In both cases, sentiment is against laws and in favor of individual choice and "natural" process. Given the earlier cynicism about the government's interest in their problems, such an attitude makes sense. If the government is seen to be unconcerned about them and their neighborhoods, then there is no reason for these women to believe that governmental decisions and actions will further their interests.

This "laissez-faire" attitude toward social change is a popular one; nevertheless, it is not applied across the board. A majority of the respondents, for example, support laws guaranteeing black families the right to buy homes wherever they choose. Three-fourths of the active women feel the government should play such a role, although a number of the women volunteer that they feel it should be a limited rather than a broad role (see Table 27). Generally, the respondents support government guarantees of freedom of movement for everyone, but not active or aggressive interference in the integration of neighborhoods. Support for the government's playing a role in open housing is greater than support for the government's taking a role in the integration of schools. This may be because the former is a _fait_ _accompli_. "There already are such laws," said one woman in response to the question. Most of the respondents are aware of the fact that open housing laws are on the books; in addition, those laws are relatively clear-cut. This contrasts with the question of school integration where the laws are still unclear, the government's actions have wavered, and the constitutional issues involved remain unresolved.

Table 27

Responses to: "Do You Think the Government Should
See to It That Black Families Can Purchase
Homes, or Should the Government Stay Out
of That?" by Activity Group

Category	Active Women		Inactive Women	
	Per-cent	N	Per-cent	N
Yes, the government should see to it	44	8	54	7
Yes, but government role should be limited	33	6	--	
The government should stay out of it	22	4	46	6
Total	99	18	100	13

The inactive women are a good deal less
supportive of government intervention in the
area of housing than are the active women.
Twice as many inactive women take the position
that the government should stay out of the business of enforcing open housing altogether. It
might be recalled that the inactive women are
also considerably less supportive of government
intervention in the area of integrating schools.
The laissez-faire, "government hands off" attitude appears to be a good deal more characteristic of the inactive women than of the active.
This suggests once again the greater political
sophistication of the active women. They are
more realistic in their willingness to accept
the fact that contemporary American government
plays an active role in determining and limiting
the extent of an individual's rights and free-
doms. Their participation in assertive community organizations shows that they are aware of
this and also concerned about seeing that some
of those decisions the government will be making
are agreeable to them and their needs.

To summarize, among the women of the

Southwest Side of Chicago, there is fairly high
verbal adherence to the idea of racial integration. At the same time, there are certain qualifications consistently applied: no governmental policy for integrating should be forced
on people; blacks should not make gains through
acting aggressively; and whites should not have
to give up their neighborhoods or be in a
numerical minority.   There is surprisingly
little difference between the active and the inactive women, although the actives emerge as
slightly more liberal, especially in the area of
personal interaction with blacks.   The active
women are also more supportive of the government's playing some role in assuring that blacks
are able to purchase homes and attend integrated
schools; they are, further, more able to spell
out the kind of role they wish the government to
play. Underlying many of these racial attitudes
is resentment, a resentment at being expected to
sympathize with and support other groups at the
very time when all they have struggled for, both
in terms of material gains and moral certitudes,
is being jeopardized.

Attitudes toward black people are inextri-
cably mixed in the minds of most Americans with
attitudes toward the poor.   These women are no
exception.   The issue of public housing provides
a focal point around which Southwest Side residents' anxieties about both black people and
poor people living in their community come together.   It was mentioned earlier that a Federal
Court decision had, just prior to the time of
the interviews, ordered that additional public
housing units be constructed in white neighborhoods in order to facilitate economic and racial
integration throughout the city.   Although no
such units had been built at the time of the
interviews, people had some idea of the designated sites and there was widespread unhappiness
with the prospect of such housing.

The only women who showed strong support
for the court decision were those living
farthest east in the neighborhood that adjoins
the black community.   Because some black

families already live in this neighborhood, no
public housing units are scheduled for the area.
If public housing were to go up west of them,
these women feel "it would take some of the
pressure off" their neighborhood. If black
families are living throughout the Southwest
Side, rather than concentrated in the eastern
section, "there will be no place for people to
run to."

Although the other residents are almost
uniformly opposed to public housing, they generally explain their opposition in terms other
than racial ones. The dominant themes which run
through the arguments against the construction
are: 1) equity, that is, the fairness of this
decision and 2) socioeconomic integration, that
is, whether or not it is a good thing to have
poor people--those who need public housing--
living in a neighborhood with families that are
better off.

The equity argument has two dimensions.
The position taken most frequently is that such
a plan could operate fairly only if the public
housing units were built throughout the city and
suburbs and not concentrated in working-class
neighborhoods. "I do think that they should be
everywhere," says one woman in explaining her
only objection to the plan. "There's none on
Judge Austin's block* or Mayor Daley's block.
. . . That's the only way, first of all, that it
would be accepted and, second, I think this is
how you're eventually going to get your
balance."

The women feel that once again a government
plan is being imposed on them by others who have
more power. They resent both the plan and their
exclusion from the decision-making process.

I think it's an infringement on my rights as a citizen
and a taxpayer . . . because I feel I have no say. I

_____

*Judge Austin is the federal court judge
who handed down the decision on future public
housing units.

feel that I am buying my home; I am paying for it; I
am keeping it up; I am paying taxes on it; and the
community around me is doing likewise. And CHA will
be public housing where the people that will live
there will not own the property; they will do as they
damn well please with the property and they will drag
the neighborhood down.

This woman expresses well the other argument that residents make in the name of
fairness: community residents should have some
say in deciding if and where public housing will
be constructed in their neighborhood.   This
argument has a ring of justice to it; the idea
of community residents participating in
decisions about their community seems fair. Yet
no one notes that black communities have never
been asked or allowed to participate in such decisions about public housing when it affects
their neighborhoods.

The equity argument laid out in these discussions carries further the point made earlier
by the women when they were asked if people in
their social class are treated unfairly. Here,
too, respondents express the feeling that they
are the victims of unfair treatment: they are
being asked to carry the burden of integrating
poor families, many of whom will be black, into
their neighborhoods and, furthermore, they are
not being given the opportunity to participate
in the decision about how that is to be done.
They do not express the injustice they feel in
social class terms.   The very word "class"
carries certain connotations uncomfortable to
the respondents.   Nonetheless, they feel an
assault is being waged on the freedom of people
like them and they feel the impotence of their
group to resist.

The second theme running through the discussion of public housing is one which supports
segregation on the basis of social class. A
strong antipathy toward poor people, both black
and white, emerges in the discussion of public
housing.   One woman fears that if the court
decision goes through, "a wrong class might get
into where they don't belong and the neighbor-

hood could turn out, not bad, but they could do damage, ruin the area. Certain groups have worked to keep a community nice and another group just shouldn't come in . . . they should have their own community."

Such antipathy toward the poor derives at least partly from a fear of "going back," as one woman put it. These families are not wealthy, and they have little financial security. They realize that they could easily, in times of financial stress, fall into a more marginal existence. There is anxiety that this could happen more readily--or at least the threat could be more close at hand--if others who are poor already are living in the neighborhood. Many of these women express great pride in the fact that there are no poor people now living in their neighborhoods. "Everyone here is doing okay." Being surrounded by families of relatively secure economic standing helps them feel more secure themselves. Conversely, being surrounded by economically marginal families serves as a constant reminder of the possibility of reverting to such a condition. As Richard Parker expresses it: "To feel constantly pressured from 'below,' to be constantly reminded of the world from which many came and to which one might so easily return, can be a traumatizing experience for those living on the edge as so many blue-collarites do."[2]

One woman speaks of how unfair she feels it is when families like hers must live with others who are less well off:

> I was always taught to better yourself as you go through life . . . never downgrade your life, always try to improve it. So, when you're thrown in with a bunch of hillbillies or a bunch of people who have no concept of how you've always lived, it's not fair either. It isn't. I'm not my brother's keeper that I have to teach her how to put garbage out just because she was able to buy a house next to me. You understand what I mean? It's going back. You just keep downgrading, going back.

The way to resolve this unfairness, many of

the women feel, is to maintain different neighborhoods for different groups. The woman who
advocates dividing the city in two, with one
half for blacks and one half for whites, also
claims "rich people shouldn't mingle with
working people" and is an extreme example of
those who hold this view. But the belief that
social order derives from racial and class
groups staying in their own spheres and keeping
their distance from each other emerges as one
deeply felt by many of the women.

　　The reaction of the respondents to the possibility of public housing in their community
is, taken in the aggregate, a complex one.
There is clearly a strong element of resistance
to the idea of black people living in the area.
Yet, as we saw earlier, most of the women are,
or at least claim to be, willing to live in integrated neighborhoods (that is, willing to live
in a neighborhood where a numerical minority of
the residents are black), but that definitely
means with black families of comparable economic
standing.

　　There are other elements that add to the
women's resistance toward the public housing
units. Resentment toward having something
forced on them by those in power is one such
element. An uneasiness at the proximity of poor
families is another. This last element is one
which is often overlooked by social scientists
and other observers of white working-class communities. It is not so readily evident and
articulated as are "anti-black sentiments" and
"feelings of powerlessness." Nonetheless, it is
a crucial factor.

　　When asked directly, these women express
with some intensity the belief that people in
their social class are treated unfairly. But,
simultaneously, they emerge as strong supporters of the very social class system they
believe is treating them unjustly. When asked
if they see anything wrong with having different
social classes in a country where everyone is
supposed to be equal, only one inactive woman
says yes, "because I like to take people for

what they are." A few women are uncertain, and
a few cannot evaluate the phenonmenon because it
is, to them, "just a fact of life." A majority
among both the active and inactive groups, however, claim there is nothing wrong with having
different social classes. In fact, there is
strong support for the existing social class
system.

Much of the support for the existence of
social classes is based on the belief that one's
class position is a reflection of how hard one
has worked: those who work harder are entitled
to more of the rewards of life. Those who do
not work so hard, on the other hand, do not deserve to get ahead. "I don't see anything wrong
with social classes," says one active woman.
"If you do the work, you get paid for it. It's
not fair to have one person working his fanny
off and have somebody else not working and them
both getting the same amount of money."

The class system is not seen as one based
on vested power, inherited fortunes, and government decisions favorable to the corporate rich.
Rather, the idea of social classes connotes
something much more immediate: those who are
somewhat better off and those who are somewhat
less well off. One's rank in this class system
is seen as the direct result of how hard one has
worked. If a woman and her husband are making
it, it is because they have worked hard; if they
are not making it, they just have not tried hard
enough. Such a view of the class structure puts
the burden of success and the shame of failure
squarely on the individual.[3] There is no recognition that the institutions of the social
system guarantee wealth and power to some groups
just as readily as they guarantee their absence
to other groups.

In line with this, struggling to reach certain goals is seen as a good thing and competition itself is felt to be healthy. The struggle
and the competition would be eliminated, it is
believed, if there were no higher social classes
to which one could aspire. "If we were all in
the same social class . . . no rich and no poor,

well, I think it would be a poor state of
affairs if there were no competition. It would
become as a tool, just working and no further
attainment. This way, you can have, you have to
have further goals." A social class system is
seen as providing indicators of mobility, signs
of how far up the ladder one has advanced.

How can this support of a social class
system which demands that the working class provide the labor yet reap minimally of the profits
be reconciled with the earlier recognition that
people like them, people in their social class,
are treated unfairly? Such divergent opinions
evidence an internal inconsistency on the part
of the respondents. Yet it is not an inconsistency unique to this sample. Indeed, Michael
Mann, in his study of value consensus in the
United States and Britain, found many such
examples of a parallel value inconsistency on
the part of working-class men and women.[4]

The women's arguments in support of the
existing social class system represent what Mann
calls "normative acceptance" of the "dominant
values." When the women claim that those who
work harder deserve more of society's rewards
and that struggling to move up the ladder and
compete with others is healthy, they are
adhering to values "promulgated by ruling groups
to legitimate their rule." Mann found in his
secondary analysis of results of empirical
studies of the working class that there was
little support for political action to change
the social structure.

> Very few of one working-class sample want wealth
> equally divided, only about half of another mixed-
> class sample think that large inequalities are wrong,
> but in a third working class sample there is con-
> sensus in favor of reducing class differentials (one
> possible explanation of the last finding is that
> 'class' is such an unpopular term that almost every-
> one is in favor of reducing it).[5]

Yet what about the women's anger over how
unfairly they are treated in this society? Such
a belief constitutes a "deviant value," that is,

a value that would be and is put forth by groups contesting the legitimacy of the existing stratification system. Why is there a questioning of the legitimacy of the social structure at this level? Again Mann's insights are useful. "Deviant values are more likely to be endorsed," he claims, "if they are presented as relevant to respondents' everyday lives."[6] When the women were asked if they are treated unfairly, they could--and did--respond immediately in terms of concrete daily hardships they are suffering. They showed adherence to a deviant value by expressing the belief that everyone is not treated equally. When asked a more abstract question about support for a society-wide social class system, on the other hand, there is verbal adherence to the dominant values. This represents an inconsistency, an inability to relate concrete experience to more abstract values, or as Mann notes, to translate that concrete experience into support for radical politics.

This inability is not due so much to their lack of training in thinking about abstract issues as to the fact that discussion about the existence of a social class system in America makes people uncomfortable. For a long time, most Americans, including social scientists, preferred to think that the United States did not have a class system in the same sense that other countries do. Any discussion of "social class" was deemed Marxist in origin and, consequently, un-American. Many Americans still exhibit such discomfort. An unwillingness to explore the issue precludes emerging with a consistent set of values.

Mann suggests another explanation when he argues that the better question might be, Why not inconsistency? Converse found that relatively few people have consistent political ideologies and the ones who do are the ones for whom such internal consistency is relevant and important, that is, those who are actively involved in the political system.[7] There is little reason, Mann argues, for those who do not actually share in societal power to develop a consistent set of societal values. Even those respondents who are most active in the organizations, who have most contact with the political system, have little sense of sharing in societal power.

The women, then, do not express a desire to eliminate the existing system of stratification. They identify it as a source of incentive and drive for people. At the same time, they evidence little personal desire to move further up the ladder themselves. Many, of course, have already experienced some increase in financial security over what their parents lived with, but expressions of further mobility aspirations are noticeably absent. Almost none of the women, as noted earlier, want to move out of their communities. When they speak of moving, it is seldom viewed as a means of bettering themselves; rather, it is seen as a necessity they would rather avoid. Most of these women are not young; their average age is thirty-nine. While 39-year-old men and women in professional careers can look forward to another ten or fifteen years of advancement in terms of income, occupational responsibility, and prestige, the blue-collar worker at this age has generally reached the peak of his or her earning power and job promotions. These women and their husbands have likely advanced as much as they ever will and they realize it.

There are other reasons put forth in support of the class system. Many of the women believe that if social classes were eliminated, all diversity between groups and between people would be eliminated as well.

The more variety you have, the more input, the more different ideas, the more backgrounds going into something, the better it has to be . . . diversity makes life much more interesting. It would be very dull if everyone thought the same and acted the same. Definitely, different classes with different attitudes are very healthy.

Another woman feels the conflict inherent in class differences is a valuable source of

diversity.   "You have to be different," she
says.   "If everybody agreed and felt the same
way about everything, it would be such a boring
world, who'd want to live in it? At least this
way you can debate, you can talk, you can
argue."

Why is there this feeling that doing away
with social classes would lead to the homogeni-
zation of individuals?   The attitudes of many
Americans toward the social class structure are
contradictory.   On the one hand, there is a
denial that the United States, where everyone is
supposed to be equal, even has a social class
system.   On the other hand, to deny its existence is to deny diversity among people, and
diversity is believed to be good.   When the
social structure is discussed in class terms,
people often grow uncomfortable. While equality
is valued, there is a belief that a "classless"
society is the kind of society that exists in
socialist or Communist countries.   A corollary
if unarticulated belief held by some is that in
such societies citizens are stripped of their
individual character and identity.   Consequently, there is a kind of logic operative
which fears that the elimination of individual
differences will follow the elimination of
social classes.   Neither the argument nor the
premises leading up to it are made explicit.
Rather, what is expressed is actually a resistance to the idea of equality, which parallels
what Lane found in his study of working-class
men.[8]   One woman states her feelings in this
regard: "The idea that everybody is born equal
and should be on the same social standing and
should have the same amount of income is social-
istic and communistic and it's highly un-
American."

In addition to the fear of losing diversity
and the belief that some people work harder and
so deserve more, another argument for the persistence of social classes is that the separation of people into different groups is a good
thing.   Such separation allows one to define
where he or she stands in relationship to others

in the social system. This argument is applied
when respondents speak of families in public
housing "bringing down" the neighborhood. They
would prefer that the poor remain at a distance
from them. They would prefer that the boundaries between themselves and those who are poor
remain intact. The women who reject child care
centers for their own use seem to have similar
feelings. Child care centers are associated in
their minds with the poor, with mothers on welfare, not with women like themselves. They
reject child care centers for themselves. They
are not poor; they can take care of their own
children; if they should ever need some day care
services, they insist they will pay for it themselves.[9]

This argument reaches in the other direction as well; these women would like also to
keep their distance from those who are better
off than they. "I'm very happy here," explains
one woman. "I feel I'm not trying to outdo the
Joneses and the Joneses aren't trying to outdo
me. If I did move into a different . . . I
don't think I'd fit well. Where? Palos, say.
I feel as though I'm just as happy right here,
without trying to outdo anybody."

What appears to be at the root of this need
to maintain order and keep people, including
themselves, in designated areas is a desire for
stability, a longing for a social world which
can be related to in terms which are readily
understood. More important than moving into a
better neighborhood, and certainly more realistically sought, is securing what one has.

Looking at these various strands of
attitudes toward the social class system,
what conclusions can be drawn about the extent of class consciousness among these
respondents? Following the distinction Leggett
has made,[10] the elements of class consciousness can be divided into those that are cognitive and those that are evaluative.

The cognitive aspect refers to whether workers
utilize class terms, identify with their class, and

display an awareness of the allocation of wealth
within the community or society. The evaluative
aspect refers to the extent to which workers think in
terms of class struggle in order to achieve class
goals.[11]

With respect to the cognitive aspect, there
is little class verbalization among the respondents; that is, they seldom spontaneously used
class terms in discussing social and political
conditions. They did see themselves as part of
a distinct socioeconomic class, although, as
seen earlier, they tend to identify that class
as "the middle class." Despite the identification of themselves as middle class, the respondents distinctly see themselves as different and separated from those who have more
money and power. Further, they possess an
awareness of how that wealth and power are
allocated; this is particularly true of the
active women. There is, then, some rudimentary
class consciousness at the cognitive level.

There is little evidence, however, of class
consciousness at the evaluative level. While
the women perceive the unfair nature of the
existing class system, they do not feel that
system should be changed. Rather, they tend to
accept the inequities they experience as an inevitable aspect of an otherwise legitimate
system. They do not think in terms of class
struggle, nor in terms of class goals. As
Leggett indicates, the evaluative aspects of
class consciousness--the awareness of being, in
Marx's terms, a class "for itself"--can only be
achieved after cognitive class consciousness
has been reached.

It is important to recognize that class
consciousness is not an all-or-nothing phenomenon, but can exist in varying degrees along a
continuum.[12] This is evidenced by the data here.
While these women are not ready to act as a
class to further their own interests, neither
are they unaware of the unfair distribution of
power and goods in the society of which they are
a part.

It is also necessary to note that Leggett, along with most analysts of the working class, focuses on male workers. A sample of women who are for the most part out of the labor market constitutes a group who have had a markedly different life experience. The isolation from neighbors which many of the women felt before they became involved in the community organizations was earlier noted. Not having close contact and communication with others in a workplace situation that is both oppressive and shared often precludes the possibility of developing class consciousness. It may be, however, that community-based organizations which focus on other kinds of oppression, allow residents to see the extent to which their plight is shared by others in their social class, and develop an analysis of the power structure may prove to be a substitute for the workplace experience for some individuals. This remains to be seen. For the present, an incipient class consciousness struggles with a desire for order, an emphasis on the individual and, ultimately, resignation. "That's the way it is, you know, some are rich and some aren't lucky enough . . . from the beginning of time it was that way. . . . There were people that had more power and were able to make more money and it just kept going that way."

Looking at the data in this chapter, there is little to suggest that the involvement of the active women derives in any substantial way from either a racist backlash or a working-class consciousness. Indeed, with respect to racial attitudes, the active women are somewhat more liberal than the inactives in supporting integrated schools and neighborhoods. They are noticeably more willing to let the government take some role in seeing that integration occurs and they are fairly articulate about what they believe that role should be. While the active women possess somewhat more progressive racial attitudes than the inactive, there is no reason to believe that such attitudes motivated their

becoming active. Rather, the ability to deal
realistically with integration and, especially,
to articulate what they believe the government's
role should be has likely grown out of shared
experiences in community organizations.

As far as attitudes toward social class are
concerned, there is virtually no difference between the activity groups in thinking that there
is anything wrong with having a class system; if
anything, the active women seem more inclined to
support the existing system. At the same time,
the most active women are considerably more
likely than those in the other groups to believe
that people in their social class are treated
unfairly.

What all this suggests is that while there
does not appear to be a distinct race or class
component motivating the involved women to
pursue their activities in the assertive community organizations, they do appear to have somewhat more complex and sophisticated analyses of
the ways in which the existence of race and
class dimensions affect them and their lives.

[IX]

New Roles
and New Communities

The preceding pages have introduced and intermittently touched on a variety of themes relevant to the involvement of working-class women in assertive community organizations.

In the course of this analysis, three major themes have emerged: first, the process of role transformation which some working-class women are experiencing; second, a new grass-roots populism; and third, the loss of community accompanied by the potential for alternative community building through assertive community organizations. These themes will be discussed both in the course of summarizing the factors found to contribute to women's becoming active and in the speculation about what appear to be the results of that activity. It was in the search for precedents and antecedents of activism that these themes emerged.

The quest of this research has been for clues which would help in answering a central question: what leads some women to become involved in community organizations with an assertive political orientation? It quickly became clear that there is a heightened political awareness and anger among the active women. More than their inactive neighbors they see serious problems in the community and they are aware of and angry about the lack of responsiveness to those problems on the part of public

officials.   It is here that the evidence for a
new strain of populism begins to emerge.

From   the   1950s   until   the   late   1960s
Americans placed increasing faith in the basic
good intentions and capabilities of the leaders
of   their   institutions--their   governments,
schools, churches, and businesses.   The sharp
awareness among white working-class people of
the   distinction   between   the   interests   of
ordinary, working people like themselves and
those few men with wealth and influence which
had   characterized   much   of   American   history
became muted during the 1950s and much of the
1960s.[1]   But in the 1970s that awareness and its
attendant anger re-emerged.   Again the real discrepancy   in   interests   was   put   in   focus.
Working-class   people   like   the   women   of   the
Southwest Side began to recognize that they have
serious problems, problems which leaders in business and government not only are not correcting
but also, in many instances, are exacerbating.
They began to realize that their neighborhoods
were being destroyed for the profits of real estate companies and politicians; their air and
water were being polluted and little was being
done by the government to stop it because large
corporations had different interests and more
clout than they; their schools were overcrowded
and doing a poor job of educating their children
because they had no organized voice to change
the priorities of their city government.   Such
problems, of course, had always existed; what
then was producing this fresh insight and anger?

First, in many ways these problems have
become more acute in recent years.   Pollution
has reached new and dangerous levels; in the
schools,   never   very   good,   overcrowding   and
tension have increased to a point which makes
any kind of learning process practically untenable; life was never very easy, but always there
was the home and the neighborhood as a final
retreat.   Now they too are being threatened,
primarily by racial change, but also through the
construction of highways, urban renewal, and
bank practices such as red-lining.

Alternative channels for grievances have also been attenuated: the local politician has been shown to be corrupt and, besides, he does not have enough power to fight the corporate interests; the local priest has often been preoccupied with resolving personal problems or dealing with political problems which speak little to the immediate needs of white working-class urban dwellers. Perhaps most important of all, in earlier years the recognition of problems was accompanied by a faith that those in positions of authority were doing what they could to resolve them. That faith is no longer there; it has been replaced by a deep distrust of those in authority and a widespread cynicism among the working and middle classes about the extent to which their problems are addressed by the government.[2]

This shift in attitudes, the growing recognition of the different class interests of different groups and the accompanying lack of trust, may provide the basis for a new populism. The most active women are characterized by the conviction that people like them, people in their social class, are being treated unfairly in this country. At the same time, this new set of attitudes is accompanied by a conviction on the part of the most active respondents that they can act to reverse this process, at least at the local level. This belief that they can wield influence and power has been fed by leaders and organizers of the assertive community organizations. Indeed, most women indicate that they did not seek out the organization but were rather sought out by someone in the group, an organizer or a friend who was a member, who urged them to participate. The belief that one can effect social change will develop only within a context of collective and shared direction.

The women of the Southwest Side see their problems with increasing clarity, although there is still a strong tendency to define them in narrow, immediate, and easily remediable terms rather than to see them as one part of a political and economic system that operates counter to their interests. They are, in effect, non-ideological. They believe that some of their interests will be realized with the proper resources, organization, time, and energy. While such convictions are essential elements of a turn toward populism, the exclusively local base and orientation of the groups whose members were interviewed give little indication of any potential support for a populist movement or candidate at the national level.[3] And, clearly, there is widespread support for the social class system as it exists. Nevertheless, there is a spirit within these groups that suggests an openness to new political demands and directions.

To round out the political profile of the most active women, it should be noted that they were more likely than the other respondents to concede that women are victims of systematic oppression in the United States. When asked directly whether women are treated unfairly, it will be recalled, 88 percent of the very active women said yes. Despite the strength of this response, there are not enough differences among activity groups, nor is a feminist position expressed with sufficient intensity and concern, to argue that such feelings were a factor leading the women to political activism. Nevertheless, this tendency is one more indication that the women who choose to be most active may well be those who are experiencing an expanding realization of the ways in which they, in their various statuses, are being mistreated.

In the course of the investigation, sources of activism or reasons for participation which are not political in nature were also uncovered. Most of these are considered and will be discussed as structural reasons. There is, however, one other variable, neither political nor structural, which emerged: the emotional attachment to their neighborhood which was found to be characteristic of the active women. The most active women had not lived in the neighborhood as long as the less active nor did they have as many relatives living nearby, yet their

desire to remain there and their feelings of
loyalty and attachment to it are stronger than
those of the group that has more familial ties.

Such feelings of neighborhood attachment
touch on another of the major themes of this
analysis, the loss of a community. Only two or
three of the women, regardless of political per-
suasion and activity, were eager to move from
their neighborhoods; but the active women were
far more likely to feel unambiguously sad about
leaving. Fear of losing their community, one to
which they have especially strong attachments,
may be a factor motivating some women to become
involved in resolving the local problems that
threaten that community. There is a suggestion
that it might have this effect, and certainly
the possibility warrants further investigation.
A stronger case, however, can be made for
arguing that the impact is in the other direction, that is, that activity in community organizations itself generates neighborhood attachment. Further discussion of the community and
the impact of its loss, from this perspective,
will come later.

The structural variables which appear to
influence participation can be viewed essentially as constraints. Certain kinds of behavior are more difficult to engage in when
certain conditions are present. Conversely,
some behaviors can be assumed more readily when
certain structural conditions are removed.

At the most fundamental level there are two
constraints on a woman's becoming intensely involved in the activities of an assertive organization in her community. These are: holding a
paying job outside the home and having pre-
school age children at home. To say that these
are constraints is not to say that no mothers of
toddlers or no employed women are active in the
assertive community organizations. Some are.
It is to say, however, that the probability of a
woman's being active appears to increase
appreciably if both of these constraining
factors are removed.

Other constraints on the women's activities emanate from their husbands. If a man is not at least minimally supportive of his wife's participation, she will not, it appears, be very likely to get involved with the group. A number of active women spoke of neighbors who had both the requisite time and concern but were not active because their husbands would not "allow" it. "He just puts his foot down," says one, of her neighbor's husband. And why does the woman give in to such a dictum? "To keep peace in the house, I guess."

It becomes clear that most active women have some support from their husbands; this is evidenced by the fact that most husbands are at least nominal members of the groups in which their wives are participants. Although husbands provide support, or at least impose no restraints on their wives' behavior, this does not in any way mean they are uniformly enthusiastic about their wives' activities. Often the time and energy a woman puts into the organization is resented by her spouse and becomes the source of tension in the marriage. Still, the husbands of the most active women at least do not forcefully impose restraints on their wives' behavior.

One other variable of not unexpected importance is the education of the husband. The active women are more likely to have husbands who have completed high school. More educated men may be less threatened by their wives' choosing to play roles outside the home. The word "choosing" is used intentionally because less educated men are more likely to be married to women who work outside the home for pay, but this is defined as a necessity, not as a willfully chosen extrafamilial role. Komarovsky noted the impact of education in determining the life style and marital roles of the blue-collar families she interviewed.[4] The evidence here reaffirms this, but suggests the education of the husbands may be a more variable and crucial factor in some situations than the education of the wives.

There is another less expected and less direct way in which the men's lives have an impact on their wives' participation: where the parents of the men live. The presence close at hand of a man's parents appears to have an inhibiting effect on a woman's participation in community organizations. The most active women were considerably more likely than the inactive to have in-laws who did not live in the same house or in the same neighborhood. This suggests that it is probably easier for a woman to move into nontraditional behavior if she is not bound by the normative constraints of a tight social network. No active woman mentioned the residence of her in-laws as a factor influencing her behavior, and likely this is something of which participants are not conscious. It seems plausible, however, that the proximity of a man's parents--if those parents come out of a traditional mold--could be an inhibiting influence on a woman, either directly or indirectly through their influence on her husband. What is less clear is why a woman's own parents do not have a like impact on her behavior. The whole area of social networks, their constituents and their degree of looseness, is one which warrants further investigation if an understanding of the latent factors which make role expansion a difficult process is to develop.

The uprooting of established social networks is an inevitable by-product of the dissolution of urban neighborhoods. While families who have moved make strong attempts to preserve the old networks over new distances, it is unlikely that they can persist with anything approaching their old level of intensity. Consequently, the earlier normative overlay, so strong because of its numerous interpenetrations, will weaken. One anticipated consequence of this attenuation is that men and women will find it easier to try out new social roles or new variants of old roles. This is likely to be one result of the loss of old communities and the movement into new.

The question of what leads some women into activity is a crucial one. A number of factors emerged in this analysis as possible contributors to that process for women on the Southwest Side. The women most likely to become very active are those who see problems in their community, do not see a response to those problems forthcoming from public officials, and believe that women like themselves can resolve the problems. They have had the experience, one which is probably essential for most potential joiners, of being brought into the group by an organizer or an otherwise already active participant. The active women are convinced that people like them, those in their social class, are treated unfairly, and they possess an intense emotional attachment to the neighborhoods in which they live. The absence of small children, a recalcitrant husband, and the demands of a paying job all remove constraints. And, finally, a relatively loose social network, one in which her in-laws live at least at some slight distance, provides a context of greater freedom and openness for experimenting with new behaviors.

The second central question of the research has been: what are the effects of participation in the assertive community organizations on the women involved? This research began with the expectation that such activism would have an impact on the participants--in some cases, a profound impact was expected.

Summarizing, there are four areas in which there is some evidence that activism has produced change: 1) the political consciousness of the participants; 2) the feelings of self-esteem which the women possess; 3) the women's relationships with their husbands; 4) the women's feelings about their community. Each will be briefly discussed.

Political consciousness. It has been noted that most active women have a stronger sense of political efficacy than the inactive; that is, they share a conviction that what they do can make a difference in the local situation. This may indeed be one of the elements which led to their decision to become active. It may also, of course, reflect one of the results of participating in an assertive community organization. A woman is likely to feel she can have an impact when she is working with others who share her convictions; this will be especially true within an organization which has had some victories. The participants develop a sense of potential power, a belief that if they work together they can achieve their goals. While this conviction is often untested and/or unfounded, it may well be essential to sustain a high level of organizational commitment.

At the same time, and somewhat paradoxically, the active women also evidence more cynicism with respect to the intentions and abilities of public officials. Whether the cynicism was present to some extent prior to the decision to participate is not clear, but certainly the cynicism has been further developed by experiences the women have had in their organizations. An actual confrontation with public or corporate officials does much to weaken the mystique which often surrounds expertise or power. Similarly, the experiences the women have had in researching the workings of government agencies and the ways in which policies are determined have fed those feelings of cynicism.

More important than the extent of feelings of efficacy or cynicism--these are, after all, difficult to determine as clear antecedents of participation--is the message that comes through strongly and directly from the women involved: their participation has succeeded in making them more political.

It seems whenever we get together, we'll say, there's going to be no civic material discussed, right? We all agree, but I just want to say, did you see this latest bill that's going to be passed in Washington? And we're off and running. It's impossible. It seems we're happiest when we're discussing these things because they are close to our hearts.

Once again the likelihood that the most active women were more political than the inactive before they joined the organization must be noted.   Nonetheless, there remains little doubt that the participation itself has had a politicizing effect on the women.   "I'd rather talk to people who are informed, who know what's going on . . . that's who I mix with now, people that know what's going on." Most of the women, in fact, are fairly self-conscious about the extent to which they are now more engaged in reading, talking, and thinking about political matters.

Further political effects of participation over time can be expected.   The active women, for example, might become involved in working on campaigns of candidates for political office. Indeed, it would not be surprising to find some of the most active women running for office themselves.   Additional research would be valuable in determining the precise nature and extent of the political impact of participation in organizations of this nature.

Self-esteem. Many women expressed the fact that, as a result of their participation, they had undergone personal as well as political changes.   Change seemed especially dramatic in the area of the participants' self-esteem. Keeping in mind that many of these women, housewives and mothers for years, had not previously had the experience of testing their competencies in the outside world, one can sense the trepidation with which they must have approached their first tasks of giving reports and assuming organizational responsibilites.   One can also sense the feelings of elation which must have accompanied the confronting and meeting of these challenges.

The first time I made a public statement . . . . I always had this kind of feeling that man is better informed, a better speaker. And it was that public hearing, and I got a public ovation and I thought, by God, I did that just as well as any man could have. And you know when you first do something, like in politics I was put in a position where people were

> depending on me and you figure, dammit, I must be on
> the ball. People were coming to me and asking me for
> help. I mustn't be so stupid.

Experiments in social psychology have
shown that women in general do have higher expectations of failure than men and are often
more willing to attribute authority and expertise to men than to women.[5] Such feelings have
been found to exist among college students and
college graduates, women whose abilities, at
least in the areas of writing, research, and
speaking skills, have been acknowledged and re-
warded to some extent. The women in these organizations are not college graduates and never
had the opportunity to develop these particular
skills and yet they were thrust into situations
calling for them. It is of little wonder that
the acquisition of such new skills and their
recognition as valuable to the group and the
community would provide a basis for the women's
developing stronger positive feelings about
themselves.

There are concrete ways in which these new
feelings of self-respect are exhibited. One
woman speaks freely of how she lost forty pounds
because she once again felt proud of herself;
for her, self-esteem was reflected in renewed
concern with her physical appearance. Speaking
of activity in her organization she says: "I
think it has really helped a lot of us to really
come out of any type of shell we have." A loss
of interest in one's appearance frequently ac-
companies intense depression or social isolation. Thus, it would not be unanticipated that
a woman overcoming feelings of depression and
isolation in her life would begin to evidence
more concern with her appearance.

Another woman mentioned that she had recently gone to her doctor for a physical examination "and when my doctor examined me, he said,
'What are you doing?' And I said, 'Fighting the
Establishment.' And he said, 'Oh, that's good;
you're in better emotional health than you've
been for a long time.'" This woman is expressing
something slightly different. The channel she

has found to express and work through her grievances has kept her from bottling up feelings of frustration and, as a result, her "emotional health" has improved. This is not, however, unrelated to self-esteem; this woman's activities have led her to feel better in general, and to feel better about herself in particular.

It is not being suggested here that women join assertive community organizations for socio-emotional reasons. What is being suggested is that participation in groups that are carrying out exciting and challenging activities, especially if that participation is of a sort that allows the participants to feel that they personally are doing worthwhile work, will have socio-emotional consequences. This study provides no indication of how long such buoyant effects will persist. It may be a "first-flush" phenomenon with a limited life or it may be the basis for feelings that will last as long as they are reinforced.

Most of the socio-emotional effects of organizational activity that were evident were positive. This was not,however,uniformly true. One woman speaks of increased anxiety, tension, and a weight gain as a result of her participation.

> You come home from meetings and you're like this [she holds out her hand, shaking it to indicate nervousness] and you can't go to sleep and you sit up for two hours to unwind, and eat. You just can't shut that off when you walk out of a hall--everything is spinning in here and I have to have a big bowl of popcorn or something.

It would not be accurate to say that the feelings this last woman expresses are altogether negative in terms of her perceptions of herself or her mental health. Meeting challenges and experiencing changes--positive long-range goals--often produce just the kinds of anxieties of which she speaks. As with the more evidently positive effects, it is difficult to estimate the long-range impact.

Changes in the marital relationship. As
we have seen, participation in assertive
community organizations seems to have a positive
impact on a woman's feelings about herself. In
addition, her concern about how she presents
herself partly derives from and partly
contributes to new friendships with men. Such
friendships, while clearly an enriching force in
an individual's life, also have the potential
for introducing strain into the marital relationship. This is especially the case among
women like those in the sample because, as
Komarovsky notes, cross-sex friendships are
neither common nor encouraged within the working
class.[6] Some women spoke of feelings of jealousy
which their husbands expressed when they saw
their wives developing friendships with male
colleagues in the organizations. One woman
half-jokingly spoke of how her husband is referred to as "the chaperone" for the women on the
block whose husbands do not attend meetings.
The fact that priests play leadership roles in
some groups tended to diffuse but not dispel
such sentiments on the part of husbands.

There are other reasons, too, why husbands
may object to their wives' new activities. In a
concrete way, more time spent with the community
organization means less time spent tending to
those at home. Meals may be a little late, the
house may be a bit less tidy, and husbands and
children may have to assume some of the domestic
burdens. If the time spent with the organization is extreme--"the week before the convention, it got to the point where I was leaving
here at nine or ten in the morning and not
getting back until eleven at night"--husbands
may feel their needs are being neglected. Even
a husband who is sympathetic to what his wife is
doing may seek to limit the amount of her participation. "One of his favorite expressions,"
says one very active woman, "is 'can't anybody
else do it?'"

The power relationship in a marriage is a
dynamic relationship.[7] When a woman is pregnant or has young children, especially when she

does not have an independent source of income,
she is particularly powerless in a marriage
because of the extent to which she is
emotionally and economically dependent on her
husband. If she gets a job and has the potential to support herself, she will gain in power
within the marriage because some of what she
gains by holding the marriage together is no
longer unattainable elsewhere. Similarly, when
she recognizes the desirability of activities
outside the home and begins participating in
them, her life in non-domestic areas will take
on new importance and, consequently, she may
become less dependent on the marital relationship for meeting all her needs. A realization
of this at some unarticulated level may be a
source of concern to some husbands.

     One context for viewing what happens as
working-class women move into new extrafamilial
roles and develop a sense of their own competence and their own ability to function independently in these roles is family power.   It
certainly does not seem farfetched to speculate
that the reason some men "put their foot down"
is because such new activities on the part of
their wives pose too much of a threat to the
established routine. One woman summed it up in
speaking of the ways in which her new life has
affected her husband: "Now he has to adjust to
a new reality."

     A few women clearly indicate that their new
activites, by expanding the scope of their world
and creating in them a new set of expectations
and demands, have led them to question the satisfaction they derive from their marriages.
Others, however, note an effect in quite the
opposite direction. One woman whose husband
shares her organizational activities speaks of
how pleased she is that they are able now to
work together on community projects. She feels
that both of them have grown through their new
friendships and interests and been brought
closer together. Another feels that, although
her husband does not share in her activities, he
has developed a new respect for her and her
abilities. "I feel now, we talk differently.

He listens to me." This has added a dimension to their relationship, and one which pleases the respondent. It is also, clearly, another way in which an active woman's feelings of self-esteem can be enhanced.

In sum, there are definite ripples of change in the relationships of the active women with their husbands. In some cases, such changes are threatening to the marriages; in other cases, they are forging new bonds between the marriage partners.

Feelings of community attachment. Attitudes about the community of residence are the fourth area in which change as a result of active participation is evident. When problems begin to confront a neighborhood, residents can respond in one of three ways. First, "they can resign themselves to the situation and, doing nothing, just tolerate it . . . or they can leave the neighborhood altogether, or they can stay and make some attempt to change things."[8] The active women are, obviously, the ones who are choosing to fight rather than flee. For this reason it was expected that they would show significantly stronger attachments to their neighborhoods than the inactive women. This turned out to be true in one sense: they were emotionally more attached to and felt more strongly about staying in the neighborhood. They did not, however, have deeper roots in the community; in fact, the inactive women had lived in their neighborhoods longer and had more relatives living there than the active women.

Women with fewer material roots in the community can have stronger emotional attachments because the experience in the organization itself produces such strong sentiments. This argument derives directly from what the women say: "At this point," says one woman, "I would feel badly about leaving the neighborhood. A year ago, I wouldn't have. But I've met so many interesting people through the group . . . . We've met people that live on the next block that we didn't know before." Working together around community issues not only has been a way for women (and their husbands) to meet other neighbors, but also seems to be a process that cements friendships:

> It's not just real serious business where you're out there reforming society. . . . We have parties to-gether and that's unusual here. . . . The whole social life is the family, the baptisms, the mar-riages, visiting Ma and Pa. . . . We've gotten socially acquainted. . . . We never met each other on this level before.

What seems to be developing, at least in some of the assertive community organizations, is a sense of communion, "for communion is formed by an actual experience of common feeling."[9] Working together intensely around mutual concerns over a period of time there develops in participants strong shared feelings and these are the essence of communion, in Schmalenbach's sense.

Communion exists in contrast to community. Community "is typically marked by a certain qui-etness and persistence. It is a structure taken for granted[10]. . . only through contrasts and disturbances does a community become an object of attention for its members."[11] These women have lived in communities. They have lived with their families, those of their own religion, and those of their own ethnic background. They have lived in a taken-for-granted world. Feelings of attachment to others have existed as a by-product of that community structure. But some-thing different is occurring now. While the assertive community organizations were begun for concrete and instrumental reasons, close emotional bonds have developed among members, and there is some indication now that feelings are the essential elements that hold the group together. It is certainly the communal feelings developed within the group, rather than the attraction of the community per se, that is keeping many of the women in the neighborhood.

The kind of assertive community organiza-tions examined here seem to have the capacity for creating strong communal bonds. This means that there can develop an alternative to the community which was forged through generations or years of common living. Whether such an alternative institution has the capacity to persist over time or whether it develops around a crisis and then wanes remains to be seen.

Evidence has been introduced suggesting that change has come about in a number of areas of the active women's lives as a result of their participation in assertive community organizations. Their political consciousness has been heightened. They are more likely to get involved in political activities and certainly more likely to have opinions on political issues. In many cases, their self-esteem has been enhanced as they begin to develop competence in areas outside the home. The dynamics of their marriage and their expectations regarding marriage are undergoing change. And their emotional attachment to the community, as represented by their feelings for others who share their commitment to the organization, has become more intense.

All these changes, considered collectively, are a part of the role transformation that is occurring in the lives of working-class women. The experiences and social parameters of working-class women are broadening, as other recent studies also document.[12] Why is this role transformation occurring among the women in this study and, apparently, other working-class women? What has brought about the role transformation in the twenty years since Rainwater and his colleagues wrote of the "workingman's wife" and her insulated world?

There are a number of forces operating to bring about this transformation. One is the overall shift in values which the American population has experienced over the last decade or so. A major example is today's widespread acceptance of the use of contraceptives, an acceptance which marks a change especially dramatic among Catholics of the working class.[13] Divorce, too, once anathema among Catholics, is now more widely accepted and practiced among all

segments of the population.[14] Despite the conflicts which they generate, these two value
changes, at the same time, provide women with a
new source of freedom and a new leverage in
planning their own lives.

Related to this, it is likely that the
change in societal norms, male-female relationships, and women's views of themselves which
have resulted from the feminist movement have
had an impact on the lives of working-class
women, even as they consciously reject much of
the ideology of that movement. For example,
there is a strong belief among the active women
that there should be more women in public office
and that, if there were, things would be better
in this country. In 1975, a number of Chicago
women made bids for aldermanic offices and found
support in working-class neighborhoods. This
was unheard of ten years ago; it constitutes a
major change. While the women who hold these
beliefs and support these candidates may not
align themselves with the women's movement,
there seems little doubt that the change in
their behavior and attitudes owes something to
the movement and its impact on society. As
well, the women's movement has been the force
behind opening to women jobs and educational
programs which had previously been closed to
them. Many of the newly available work, study,
and training opportunities are affecting the
lives of working-class women and contributing to
the process of role transformation.

Finally, as indicated earlier, the uprooting of old neighborhoods and, along with them,
of old social networks is freeing women from
certain traditional norms and pressures. The
results of the loosening of these networks,
other than identifiable feelings of loneliness,
may not be recognized by those who are experiencing it. Nevertheless, the phenomenon is
having an impact on these women's lives and will
have an even more profound impact on their
daughters' lives.

While events over which they have no control are shaping their futures, the women who

have become involved in assertive community organizations are not passive victims of circumstances.   These women have made choices for
their lives.   They have chosen to confront what
they see as neighborhood problems.   They have
chosen to invest time in an extrafamilial role.
The decision to become involved, the persistence
in dealing with the community problems, the burden of time and energy which such activities
demand, and the willingness to readjust domestic
schedules all suggest a conscious commitment on
the part of these women to their new role.   As
part of that commitment, the active women are
engaging in behaviors which constitute breaks
with their own tradition and that of their community.   They are participating in the assertive
tactics of the organizations of which they are a
part.   Demonstrating, picketing, and confronting public officials are actions which, by the
women's own admission, they would never have
thought of engaging in a few years ago.   They
are also developing skills and competencies--in
areas such as research, public speaking, and
organizing--which are new to them.   Furthermore,
they are developing a political orientation
which does not fit the one traditionally attributed to working-class women.   They see their
candidate preferences increasingly independent
of either political party; they have made themselves well informed about the intricacies of
the political system; and, from small victories,
they have developed some feelings of political
efficacy.

     Yet the choices they are making and the
changes which accompany them are not always easy
and often raise conflicts and questions in the
women's own minds.   There are ways, however, in
which these nontraditional behaviors have been
legitimated within a traditional context.   Most
basic, perhaps, is the way in which the new concerns are perceived as an extension of traditional concerns, such as the safety of children
and the quality of neighborhood life.   Also contributing in some cases to the legitimation of
new activites is the leadership role played by
priests.   While activist priests are by no means

playing traditional clerical roles themselves,
the very fact that they are priests is likely to
aid the women in feeling more comfortable as
they take on nontraditional behaviors. The nontraditional behaviors can be assumed within a
context which, because of the guidance and
leadership of a priest, offers both familiarity
and support.

Nonetheless, anxieties persist. The most
prevalent anxiety for the women centers around
the possibility that their activities may have
some ill effects on their families. Many of the
most active women are quite sensitive to, and
even defensive about, such a possibility. They
stress the fact that their activities do not in-
terfere with meeting the demands of family and
household. They emphasize that what they are
doing they are doing for their families, and
some recurrently state that they receive no
money for their work.

This last point seems especially important
in allaying their husbands' doubts about their
activities. The fact that it is unpaid work
makes it clear that the women do not need to
earn any extra money and assures, in a society
where the "value" of work is determined by the
salary attached to it, that the primacy of the
husband's work remains unquestioned. At some
level, the women realize the importance of fore-
seeing and forestalling husbands' resistance.
It was mentioned that some men are jealous of
their wives' new friendships with men; some,
too, are jealous of their wives' time. ("He
does get aggravated sometimes. The phone will
ring, interrupt supper or something.") It is
also possible, although there are no clear indications of this, that there may be resentment on
the part of some men toward their wives' assuming the role of political expert in the family.

The experience of role conflict may help
explain the adherence of the active women to
some extremely traditional positions with
respect to what is appropriate behavior for
women. In Chapter III, the very active women
were seen as the most likely to have a negative

response to the idea of a woman's becoming
President--while, at the same time, they were
most likely to say they would vote for a woman
for President.   We also saw the most active
women emerging as most supportive of traditional
family roles for women.   More so than the less
active and the inactive women, they support
women's marrying, having children, not having
abortions, and letting men make the family decisions.   This paradox--the women whose behavior
is least traditional voicing verbal support for
the most traditional roles for women--suggests
that they are experiencing some internal conflict.

     Role strain characterizes attempts to per-
form adequately a multiplicity of roles.   It may
be just such role strain that is producing what
appear to be inconsistent attitudes among the
most active women.   To view what is happening
more positively, it is worthwhile here to point
out Sieber's recent observation that "role accumulation" often produces benefits that far out-
weigh any resultant role strain.

     . . . role accumulation may enrich the personality
     and enhance one's self-conception.   Tolerance of
     discrepant viewpoints, exposure to many sources of
     information, flexibility in adjusting to the demands
     of diverse role-partners, reduction of boredom--all
     of these benefits may accrue to the person who enjoys
     wide and varied contacts with his fellow men [sic].[15]

     Whether due to the role accumulation
process or the impact of this particular new
role, such positive effects on the lives of the
most active women are apparent.   The ones most
evident are: increased self-esteem and self-
confidence; broadened social contacts; (sometimes) improved relationships within the
family; and a new source of excitment and challenge in the lives of the participants.

     Sieber also recalls a theory of psy-
chotherapy "which asserts that a capacity to
be self-critical is enhanced by taking a number
of roles, each of which yields a particular
'me.'"[16] This brings to mind the greater

capacity to be self-critical which very active
women have.   In Chapter III, they were more
likely than either the less active or the inactive to see things in themselves which they
dislike.   They also were particularly focused on
the "unladylike" qualities they saw in themselves, such as being loud, getting angry, or
"exploding."   This certainly suggests a greater
capacity to be self-critical, although, of
course, there is no way of knowing whether such
a capacity results from the role accumulation
they have experienced or whether it existed in
this group of women prior to their involvement.

        This chapter has attempted to draw together
various themes that have emerged from the data,
to present a more unified picture of what leads
to activism and what results from it, and to
speculate on ways in which the phenomenon explored here is connected with broader changes
that are occurring in working-class communities
and in the lives of working-class women.   Conclusions have necessarily been speculative; it
was the intent of this study to propose hypotheses and raise questions that might fruitfully
be explored further.

        This study has addressed itself to a
specific community in a particular city--the
Southwest Side of Chicago.   But the questions it
raises have implications for the United States
as a whole.   Other neighborhoods in other cities
have formed assertive community organizations.
Undoubtedly, more such groups will form in the
future, and not only by the white working class,
but by every segment of society that has lost
faith in a government which--on a city-wide and
a national level alike--is seen as insensitive
to the needs of its citizens and responsive only
to powerful interest groups.   The women who
speak in these pages express an astonishing
cynicism and resentment about their elected city
officials in particular and about government in
general.   In what is so far a small way, they
are seeking to transform that government into
one more responsive to their wishes and needs.
What kind of success they will have is unclear.

But one thing seems clear already: in the process of making social change, the women too are
changing.

Notes

Introduction

    1. Amundsen, The Silenced Majority; Seifer, Absent from the Majority.
    2. Roby, "Sociology and Women in Working-Class Jobs"; Bibb, "Blue-Collar Women in Low-Wage Industries"; Baker, "Job Opportunities of Black and White Working-Class Women"; Finley, "Understanding Oppression."
    3. Social Research, Inc., "A Study of Working-Class Women in a Changing World."
    4. Seifer, Absent from the Majority.
    5. Seifer, Nobody Speaks for Me.
    6. Iglitzin, "The Making of the Apolitical Woman."
    7. Frieden, "Housing and National Urban Goals."

Chapter I. Women of the Working Class

    1. Lemon, The Troubled American; Armbruster, The Forgotten American; Coles, The Middle Americans.
    2. Levine and Herman, "Group Conflict, Group Interest, and Group Identity."
    3. Phillips, Emerging Republican Majority.
    4. Krickus, "Organizing Neighborhoods: Gary and Newark."
    5. Kotler, Neighborhood Government.
    6. Barbara Mikulski in Baltimore and Mary Lou Wolfe and Gail Cincotta in Chicago are examples of such leadership.
    7. Seifer, Absent from the Majority.
    8. Rainwater, Coleman, and Handel, Workingman's Wife, p. 26.

9. Ibid., p. 107.

10. Ibid., p. 30.

11. For a brief account of this history, see Chapter 5, "Bread and Roses," in Rowbotham, Women, Resistance and Revolution.

12. Gutman, "Work, Culture, and Society in Industrializing America."

13. Marc Fried, for one, speaks of the "deep commitment of people to their neighborhoods, and close-knit social organization within the local area" which are "among the most striking features of working-class community life." See his The World of the Urban Working Class, p. 94.

14. Friedan, The Feminine Mystique.

15. Ibid., p. 53.

16. U.S. Department of Labor, "Marital and Family Characteristics of the Labor Force, March 1974," p. A12.

17. Gold, "Woman and Voluntarism," pp. 533-554.

18. U.S. Department of Labor, op. cit.

19. Komarovsky, Blue-Collar Marriage. pp. 151-155.

20. Sexton, "Speaking for the Working-Class Wife," p. 130.

21. Rainwater, Coleman, and Handel, Workingman's Wife, p. 77.

22. Komarovsky, p. 43.

23. Ibid., p. 197.

24. Gurin, Veroff, and Feld, Americans View Their Mental Health, p. 227.

25. Ibid.

26. Langer, "Inside the Telephone Company," p. 347.

27. Gans, The Urban Villagers, p. 236.

28. Lane, Political Life, p. 215.

29. Sexton, "Wife of the Happy Worker," pp. 81-85.

30. Rainwater, Coleman, and Handel, Workingman's Wife, p. 44.

31. Sexton, "Wife of the Happy Worker," p. 82. Coleman and Neugarten, Social Status in the City, p. 176, make a similar point.

32. Booth, "Sex and Social Participation."

33. This discussion is indebted to Lopata, "The Function of Voluntary Associations in an Ethnic Community: 'Polonia'."

34. Sexton, "Speaking for the Working-Class Wife," p. 130.

35. Sexton, "Wife of the Happy Worker," p. 85.

36. For recent discussion of this issue, see: Acker, "Women and Social Stratification"; Haug, "Social Class Measurement and Women's Occupational Roles."

37. Parkin, Class Inequality and Political Order, p. 15.

38. U.S. Department of Labor, op. cit.

39. While $11,500 is higher than Chicago's 1970 city-wide median of $10,280, it must be kept in mind that these are all-white neighborhoods. In Chicago, race is a major factor in income differentials: while 73 percent of the predominantly black neighborhoods are below the city median, 78 percent of white neighborhoods are above it.

40. Community Area Data Book: Chicago, 1970.

41. The visible and controversial elements were gauged not only by discussions with various community residents, but also through an analysis of the local Southwest Side newspapers, The Southwest News-Herald and the Southtown Economist.

Chapter II. The Community: The Southwest Side of Chicago

1. Interview with Francis X. Lawlor, October 25, 1972.

2. FHA loans are given to those who wish to purchase a house but are unable to get conventional bank loans and mortgages. In Lawlor's area, a majority of the black families purchasing homes have been doing so with FHA loans.

3. Lawlor did not run for re-election to the City Council in 1975. Rather, he ran as a Republican in a special election to fill a Congressional seat. He was defeated in that election by the Democratic candidate, but has suggested he may run again.

4. For a discussion of the changes Chicago's communities have experienced in the perceptions of succeeding generations see Hunter, Symbolic Communities.

5. Local Community Fact Book: Chicago Metropolitan Area 1960. All future references to 1960 Census data will be from this source.

6. The precise figure, based on 1970 Census data, is 68.67 percent black. Community Area Data Book for the City of Chicago, p. 561. All future references to 1970 data are from this source.

7. Suttles, The Social Construction of Communities, p. 58.

8. Ibid.

9. Quotations from the interview with Southwest Side women will be used regularly to illustrate points. Any quotation not otherwise footnoted is from the interviews.

10. This explanation was set forth by a Common Counsel member on a local television show, Common Ground, on January 27, 1973.

11. For Alinsky's own description of his goals and techniques, see his Rules for Radicals.

12. Suttles, p. 62.

13. Suttles, p. 63.

14. Ibid.

15. Suttles, pp. 60-61.

16. Southwest News-Herald, April 13, 1972.

17. Irving Tallman, in his study of working-class wives who had moved to the suburbs, found that the resultant breakdown in primary group relations led to just such feelings of social isolation. See "Working-Class Wives in Suburbia."

Chapter III. Yesterday's Expectations, Today's Lives

1. Sexton, "Speaking for the Working-Class Wife."

2. Social Research, Inc., "A Study of Working-Class Women in a Changing World."

3. "Community" is used here to refer to the Southwest Side as a whole. "Neighborhood" refers to the smaller designated areas within the community, e.g., Bridgeport, Clearing, Chicago Lawn.

4. Fellman and Brandt, The Deceived Majority.

5. Davis, "Careers as Concerns of Blue-Collar Girls."

6. Sennett and Cobb, The Hidden Injuries of Class.

7. Rainwater, Coleman, and Handel, Workingman's Wife, p. 68.

8. Komarovsky, Blue-Collar Marriage, p. 149.

9. Sexton, "Speaking for the Working-Class Wife."

10. Handel and Rainwater, "Persistence and Change in Working-Class Lifestyles."

Chapter IV. Who Joins? Political Antecedents of Participation

1. As of this writing, the U.S. Court of Appeals had upheld the lower court decision, but the group

opposed to public housing had vowed to take their case to the Supreme Court.

2. See Greeley, McCready and McCourt, Catholic Schools in a Declining Church, for a study of the Catholic school system in the 1970s which addresses these specific issues.

3. Chicago is divided into fifty wards, each of which elects an alderman to sit on the City Council. The neighborhoods under consideration here are located in six wards.

4. There were two areas in which the legitimacy of the government's making decisions was questioned. These areas are sex education in the schools and the construction of public housing in the community. On these two issues the perspective is decidedly different: the community should make its own decisions and the government should not involve itself.

5. Rainwater, Coleman, and Handel, Workingman's Wife p. 44.

6. Sexton, "Speaking for the Working-Class Wife," p. 129.

Chapter V. Who Joins?   Psychological and Structural Antecedents

1. Suttles, The Social Construction of Communities, p. 40.

2. Bart, "Depression in Middle-Aged Women."

3. Other researchers note that middle-aged women are the ones most likely to become involved in volunteer work. See Gold, "Women and Voluntarism."

4. Gans, The Urban Villagers, Chapter 3 and Rainwater, Coleman, and Handel, Workingman's Wife, Chapter VI.

5. See the references in the Introduction, note 1.

6. Fellman and Brandt, The Deceived Majority; Parker, The Myth of the Middle Class.

7. Gold, "Women and Voluntarism," p. 542.

8. Burris, "Fourth World Manifesto."

9. One woman was at a loss for a response when asked if a single person could become a member of her organization. The usual pattern is for a couple to join, although one partner will often play a more active role.

10. Gans, The Urban Villagers; Hausknecht, "The Blue-Collar Joiner."

11. This is based on either one or two living

parents. Approximately 25 percent of the parents of each group of respondents are deceased.

12. Bott, Family and Social Networks.

13. Ibid., p. 59.

14. Ibid.

15. Ibid., p. 103.

16. Ibid., p. 53.

17. Ibid., p. 60.

18. Ibid.

19. Ibid., p. 54.

20. Davis, "Careers as Concerns of Blue-Collar Girls," p. 160, notes the tendency for males to have more traditional attitudes toward females even among high school students. Rossi also notes this in "Barriers to the Career Choice of Engineering, Medicine, or Science Among American Women," p. 87.

21. Weber, The Methodology of the Social Sciences, p. 90.

22. Ibid.

Chapter VI. Community Activism and the Feminist Movement

1. Chafee, The American Woman, Chapter 1.

2. Goldman, "Woman Suffrage."

3. Stone, "The Offensive."

4. Chafetz, Masculine/Feminine or Human?, p. 149.

5. Verba and Nie, Participation in America, p. 287.

6. Study Number 4119, Survey Research Service, National Opinion Research Center.

7. Gillespie, "Who Has the Power?"

8. Ibid., p. 136.

9. Rainwater and Handel, "Changing Family Roles in the Working-Class."

10. Amundsen, The Silenced Majority, p. 21.

11. Susan Jacoby in an article on a consciousness-raising group in a working-class Brooklyn community found, similarly, that women identified with selected issues of the women's movement. See "What Do I Do for the Next 20 Years?"

Chapter VII. Political Correlates of Organizational
              Participation

1. Lane, Political Life; Almond and Verba, The Civic Culture; Campbell, Converse, Miller and Stokes, The

American Voter.

2. Jennings and Thomas, "Men and Women in Party Elites."

3. Iglitzin, "Political Education and Sexual Liberation."

4. Lansing, "The American Woman."

5. Verba and Nie, Political Participation, p. 84.

6. A recent national survey, the National Opinion Research Center's General Social Survey of 1974, found 32 percent of a cross-section of the U.S. adult population claimed to be independents. Both active women and their husbands then are well above the mean; inactive women are close to it; their husbands are well below the mean.

7. Levitt, "The Political Role of American Women."

8. Verba and Nie, Political Participation, p. 31.

9. Campbell, Gurin, and Miller, The Voter Decides, p. 206.

10. Verba and Nie, Political Participation, p. 186.

11. All of the groups are non-partisan in the sense that they do not actively campaign for or promote a single candidate as an organization. Clearly, though, they have their favorites. The office of one organization, for instance, had literature publicly displayed and available for distribution which supported one candidate for State's Attorney.

12. Verba and Nie, Political Participation, p. 186.

13. Campbell, Gurin, and Miller, The Voter Decides, p. 187.

14. Lane, Political Life, p. 149.

Chapter VIII.   The Bases of Division: Race and Social
                Class

1. Greeley and Sheatsley, "Attitudes Towards Desegregation." Our questions were administered in 1972; the Greeley-Sheatsley questionnaire was administered in 1970.

2. Parker, The Myth of the Middle Class, p. 11. Lee Rainwater makes the same argument in "Making the Good Life."

3. Sennett and Cobb, The Hidden Injuries of Class, discuss this same phenomenon.

4. Mann, "The Social Cohesion of Liberal Democracy."

5. Ibid., p. 429.

6. Ibid.
7. Converse, "The Nature of Belief Systems in Mass Publics."
8. Lane, Political Ideology, Chapter 4.
9. Child care centers, of course, are not all government-run and tax-subsidized. Yet this is the image of child care centers these women hold. The kind of center supported, controlled, and run by parents seems not familiar to them.
10. Leggett, Class, Race and Labor, p. 39.
11. Ibid.
12. Finley, "Understanding Oppression."

Chapter IX. New Roles and New Communities

1. Newfield and Greenfield, A Populist Manifesto.
2. This is evidenced by the results of the 1973 and 1974 General Social Surveys, administered to a national sample by the National Opinion Research Center. More recently, a survey by Peter Hart Research Associates showed 58 percent of the public agreeing that "local community interest and needs are not represented in making company policy" and 57 percent agreeing that "both the Democratic and Republican parties are in favor of big business rather than the average worker." Reported in Common Sense, the newspaper of the People's Bicentennial Commission, Vol. 3, Number 3.
3. Rose and Rothstein, "The Working-Class Reformers," present an analysis of the limits and potentials of one such working-class organization.
4. Komarovsky, Blue-Collar Marriage, p. 21.
5. Horner, "Women's Will to Fail"; Goldberg, "Are Women Prejudiced Against Women?"
6. Komarovsky, Blue-Collar Marriage, Chapter 9.
7. Heer, "The Measurement and Bases of Family Power"; Gillespie, "Who Has the Power?"
8. Orbell and Uno, "A Theory of Neighborhood Problem Solving."
9. Schmalenbach, "The Sociological Category of Communion."
10. Ibid., p. 338.
11. Ibid., p. 334.
12. Seifer, Absent From the Majority; Social Research, Inc., "A Study of Working-Class Women in a Changing World."
13. A recent study shows an increase in the last

decade from 45 percent to 83 percent of adult Catholics saying that a married couple who have as many children as they want are not really doing anything wrong when they use artificial means to prevent conception. Greeley, McCready, and McCourt, Catholic Schools in a Declining Church.

14. Divorce is indeed becoming more widely accepted among Catholics. The study mentioned above shows that the percentage of adult Catholics agreeing that it is all right for two people who are in love to marry even if one has been divorced increased from 52 percent in 1964 to 73 percent in 1974.

Nevertheless, there are some who still view divorce as unacceptable. The director of one assertive community organization not in this study mentioned that he believed some of the women who participate so intensely in the organization do so "to preserve their sanity"; that is, he explained, to find activity with some meaning to serve as a balance to their unhappy marriages which could not be ended because divorce was an unacceptable alternative.

15. Sieber, "Toward a Theory of Role Accumulation," p. 576.

16. Ibid.

Bibliography

Acker, Joan. "Women and Social Stratification: A Case of Intellectual Sexism " American Journal of Sociology, LXXVIII, January 1973, 936-945.

Alinsky, Saul. Rules for Radicals. New York: Random House, 1971.

Almond, Gabriel A. and Sidney Verba. The Civic Culture. Boston: Little, Brown, and Co., 1965.

Amundsen, Kirsten. The Silenced Majority. Englewood Cliffs: Prentice-Hall, Inc., 1971.

Armbruster, Frank. The Forgotten American. New York: Arlington House, 1973.

Baker, Sally Hillsman. "Job Opportunities of Black and White Working-Class Women." Social Problems, April 1975, Vol. 22, No. 4, 510-532.

Bart, Pauline B. "Depression in Middle-Aged Women" in Vivian Gornick and Barbara K. Moran, eds., Women in a Sexist Society: Studies in Power and Powerlessness. New York: Basic Books, Inc., 1971.

Bibb, Robert. "Blue-Collar Women in Low-Wage Industries: A Dual-Labor Market Interpretation." Paper presented at the American Sociological Asociation meeting, August 1975, San Francisco, California.

Booth, Alan. "Sex and Social Participation." American Sociological Review, XXXVII, April 1972, 183-193.

Bott, Elizabeth. Family and Social Networks: Roles, Norms and External Relationships in Ordinary Urban Families. New York: The Free Press, 1971.

Burris, Barbara in agreement with Kathy Barry, Terry Moon, Joann Delor, Joann Parent, Cate Stadelman, "Fourth World Manifesto" in Roberta Salper, ed.,

Female Liberation: History and Current Politics, New York: Alfred A. Knopf, 1972.

Campbell, Angus, Philip Converse, Warren Miller, and Donald Stokes. The American Voter. New York: John Wiley and Sons, 1960.

Campbell, Angus, Gerald Gurin, and Warren E. Miller. The Voter Decides. Evanston: Row, Peterson and Company, 1954.

Chafee, William. The American Woman: Her Changing Social, Economic, and Political Roles, 1920-1970. New York: Oxford University Press, 1972.

Chafetz, Janet Saltzman. Masculine/Femine or Human? Itasca: F.E. Peacock Publishers, Inc. 1974.

Coleman, Richard and Bernice Neugarten. Social Status in the City. San Francisco: Jossey-Bass, Inc., 1971.

Coles, Robert. The Middle Americans. New York: Atlantic-Little Brown and Company, 1971.

Community Area Data Book: Chicago 1970. Published by Chicago Association of Commerce and Industry and OSLA Finacial Services Corporation, Chicago.

Converse, Philip E. "The Nature of Belief Systems in Mass Publics" in David E. Apter, ed., Ideology and Discontent. Glencoe: The Free Press, 1964.

Davis, Ethelyn. "Careers as Concerns of Blue-Collar Girls" in Arthur B. Shostak and William Gomberg, eds., Blue-Collar World. Englewood Cliffs: Prentice-Hall, Inc., 1964.

Fellman, Gordon with Barbara Brandt. The Deceived Majority: Politics and Protest in Middle America. New Brunswick: Trans-Action Books, 1973.

Finley, Mary Lou. "Understanding Oppression: An Exploration of Class Consciousness and Class-Sex Consciousness Among Women Factory Workers." Paper presented at the Pacific Sociological Association meeting, March 1974, San Jose, California.

Fried, Marc. The World of the Urban Working Class. Cambridge: Harvard University Press, 1973.

Friedan, Betty. The Feminine Mystique. New York: Dell Publishing Co., 1963.

Frieden, Bernard J. "Housing and National Urban Goals: Old Politics and New Realities" in James Q. Wilson, ed., The Metropolitan Enigma: Inquiries into the Nature and Dimensions of America's Urban Crisis. Cambridge: Harvard University Press, 1968.

Gans, Herbert. The Urban Villagers. New York: The Free Press, 1962.

Gillespie, Dair L. "Who Has the Power? The Marital
     Struggle" in Hans Peter Dreitzel, ed., Family,
     Marriage, and the Struggle of the Sexes. New York:
     The Macmillan Co., 1972.
Gold, Doris. "Women and Voluntarism" in Vivian Gornick
     and Barbara Moran, eds., Women in a Sexist Society:
     Studies in Power and Powerlessness. New York:
     Basic Books, Inc., 1971.
Goldberg, Philip. "Are Women Prejudiced Against Women?"
     Trans-action, V, April 1968, 28-30.
Goldman, Emma. "Woman Suffrage" in Anarchism and Other
     Essays. New York: Dover Publications, Inc., 1969.
Greeley, Andrew, William McCready, and Kathleen McCourt.
     Catholic Schools in a Declining Church. New York:
     Sheed and Ward, 1976.
Greeley, Andrew M. and Paul B. Sheatsley. "Attitudes
     Towards Desegregation." Scientific American, CCXXV,
     December 1971, 13-19.
Gurin, Gerald, Joseph Veroff and Sheila Feld. Americans
     View Their Mental Health. New York: Basic Books,
     Inc., 1960.
Gutman, Herbert G. "Work, Culture, and Society in Indus-
     trializing America, 1815-1919." American Historical
     Review, June 1973, Vol. 78, 531-587.
Handel, Gerald and Lee Rainwater. "Persistence and
     Change in Working-Class Lifestyles" in Arthur B.
     Shostak and William Gomberg, eds., Blue-Collar
     World. Englewood Cliffs: Prentice-Hall, Inc.,
     1964.
Haug, Marie R. "Social Class Measurement and Women's
     Occupational Roles." Social Forces, LII, September
     1973, 86-98.
Hausknecht, Murray. "The Blue-Collar Joiner" in Arthur
     B. Shostak and William Gomberg, eds., Blue-Collar
     World. Englewood Cliffs: Prentice-Hall, Inc.,
     1964.
Heer, David M. "The Measurement and Bases of Family
     Power: An Overview." Marriage and Family Living,
     XXV, 1963, 133-139.
Horner, Matina S. "Women's Will to Fail." Psychology
     Today, II, March 1969, 36-38.
Hunter, Albert. Symbolic Communities: The Persistence
     and Change of Chicago's Local Communities. Chicago:
     The University of Chicago, 1974.
Iglitzin, Lynne B. "Political Education and Sexual

Liberation." <u>Politics and Society</u>, II, Winter, 1972.

Iglitzin, Lynne B. "The Making of the Apolitical Woman: Feminity and Sex-Stereotyping in Girls" in Jane S. Jaquette, ed., <u>Women in Politics</u>, New York: John Wiley and Sons, 1974.

Jacoby, Susan. "What Do I Do for the Next 20 Years?" <u>New York Times Magazine</u>, June 17, 1973.

Jennings, M. Kent and Norman Thomas. "Men and Women in Party Elites: Social Roles and Political Resources." <u>Midwest Journal of Political Science</u>, XII, November 1968, 469-492.

Komarovsky, Mirra. <u>Blue-Collar Marriage</u>. New York: Vintage Books, 1962.

Kotler, Milton. <u>Neighborhood Government: The Local Foundations of Political Life</u>. New York: The Bobbs-Merrill Co., 1969.

Krickus, Richard J. "Organizing Neighborhoods: Gary and Newark." <u>Dissent</u>, Winter 1972.

Lane, Robert E. <u>Political Life</u>. New York: The Free Press, 1959.

Lane, Robert E. <u>Political Ideology</u>. New York: The Free Press, 1962.

Langer, Elinor. "Inside the Telephone Company," in <u>Women at Work</u>, William L. O'Neil, ed., Chicago: Quadrangle Books, 1972.

Lansing, Marjorie. "The American Woman: Voter and Activist," Jane S. Jaquette, ed., New York: John Wiley and Sons, 1974.

Leggett, John C. <u>Class, Race and Labor: Working Class Consciousness in Detroit</u>. New York: Oxford University Press, 1968.

Lemon, Richard. <u>The Troubled American</u>. New York: Simon and Schuster, 1969.

Levine, Irving M. and Judith Herman. "Group Conflict, Group Interest, and Group Identity: Some Reflections on 'New Pluralism'" in Michael Wenk, S. M. Tomaski, and Geno Baroni, eds., <u>Pieces of a Dream: The Ethnic Worker's Crisis with America</u>. New York: Center for Migration Studies, 1972.

Levitt, Morris. "The Political Role of American Women." <u>Journal of Human Relations</u>, XV, January 1967.

<u>Local Community Fact Book: Chicago Metropolitan Area, 1960</u>. Evelyn M. Kitagawa and Karl E. Taeuber, eds., Chicago: University of Chicago, 1963.

Lopata, Helena Znaniecki. "The Function of Voluntary
    Associations in an Ethnic Community: 'Polonia'" in
    Ernest W. Burgess and Donald J. Bogue, eds., Contri-
    butions to Urban Sociology. Chicago: University of
    Chicago Press, 1964.

Mann, Michael. "The Social Cohesion of Liberal Demo-
    cracy." American Sociological Review, XXXV, June
    1970, 423-439.

Newfield, Jack and Jeff Greenfield. A Populist Manifesto:
    The Making of a New Majority. New York: Warner
    Paperback Library, 1972.

Orbell, John M. and Toru Uno. "A Theory of Neighborhood
    Problem Solving: Political Action vs. Residential
    Mobility." American Political Science Review, LXVI,
    June 1972, 471-489.

Parkin, Frank. Class Inequality and Political Order. New
    York: Praeger Publications, 1971.

Parker, Richard. The Myth of the Middle Class. New York:
    Liveright, 1972.

Phillips, Kevin. The Emerging Republican Majority. New
    Rochelle: Arlington House, 1969.

Rainwater, Lee. "Making the Good Life: Working-Class
    Family and Life Styles" in Sar A. Levitan, ed.,
    Blue-Collar Workers: A Symposium on Middle America.
    New York: McGraw Hill, Inc. 1971.

Rainwater, Lee, Richard P. Coleman,and Gerald Handel.
    Workingman's Wife: Her Personality, World and Life
    Style. New York: Oceana Publications, 1959.

Rainwater, Lee and Gerald Handel. "Changing Family Roles
    in the Working Class" in Arthur B. Shostak and
    William Gomberg, eds., Blue-Collar World. Englewood
    Cliffs: Prentice-Hall, Inc., 1964.

Roby, Pamela. "Sociology and Women in Working-Class
    Jobs," in Marcia Millman and Rosabeth Moss Kanter,
    eds., Another Voice: Feminist Perspectives On
    Social Life and Social Science. New York: Anchor
    Press, 1975.

Rose, Don and Richard Rothstein. "The Working-Class
    Reformers." The Nation, September 21, 1974, 239-243.

Rossi, Alice. "Barriers to the Career Choice of
    Engineering, Medicine, or Science Among American
    Women" in Jacqueline A. Mattfeld and Carol G. Van
    Aken, eds., Women and the Scientific Professions.
    Cambridge: The M.I.T. Press, 1965.

Rowbotham, Sheila. Women, Resistance and Revolution. New
    York: Vintage Books, 1972.

Schmalenbach, Herman.   "The Sociological Category of
    Communion" in Talcott Parsons, Edward Shils, Kasper
    D. Naegle, Jesse R. Pitts, eds., Theories of
    Society: Foundations of Modern Sociological Theory.
    New York: The Free Press, 1961.
Seifer, Nancy. Absent from the Majority: Working-Class
    Women in America. New York: American Jewish Com-
    mittee, 1973.
Seifer, Nancy. Nobody Speaks for Me: Self-Portraits of
    American Working-Class Women. New York: Simon and
    Schuster, 1976.
Sennett, Richard and Jonathan Cobb. The Hidden Injuries
    of Class. New York: Vintage Books, 1973.
Sexton, Patricia Cayo. "Speaking for the Working-Class
    Wife." Harper's Magazine, October 1962.
Sexton, Patricia Cayo. "Wife of the Happy Worker" in
    Arthur B. Shostak and William Gomberg, eds., Blue-
    Collar World.   Englewood Cliffs: Prentice-Hall,
    Inc., 1964.
Sieber, Sam D. "Toward A Theory of Role Accumulation."
    American Sociological Review, XXXIX, August 1974.
Social Research, Inc. A Study of Working-Class Women in a
    Changing World. Chicago, 1973.
Stone, I. F. "The Offensive: Machismo in Washington."
    The New York Review of Books, May 18, 1972, 13-14.
Suttles, Gerald. The Social Construction of Communities.
    Chicago: University of Chicago Press, 1972.
Tallman, Irving.   "Working-Class Wives in Suburbia:
    Fulfillment or Crisis?" Journal of Marriage and the
    Family, XXXI, February 1969, 65-72.
U.S. Department of Labor. "Marital and Family Character-
    istics of the Labor Force, March 1974."   Special
    Labor Force Report 173.   Washington, D.C.:
    Government Printing Office, 1975.
Verba, Sidney and Norman H. Nie.   Participation in
    America: Political Democracy and Social Equality.
    New York: Harper and Row, 1972.
Weber, Max. The Methodology of the Social Sciences.
    Glencoe: The Free Press, 1949.